Blessings All Around Us

Blessings All Around Us

Savoring God's Gifts

Dolores R. Leckey

Foreword by Bishop Robert Morneau

Resurrection Press
Mineola • New York

Dedication

For my grandchildren: Grace Marie, Cameron, Maria,
Monica, Roman and Samuel

And for children everywhere
who are our dearest blessings.

First published in 1999 by Resurrection Press, Ltd.
P.O. Box 248
Williston Park, NY 11596

ISBN 1-878718-50-9

Library of Congress Catalog Card Number 99-70152

Poems by Jessica Powers are from *The Selected Poetry of Jessica Powers*; ed. Regina
Siegfried, ASC and Robert Morneau; ICS Publications; all copyrights Carmelite
Monastery, Pewaukee, WI; used with permission.

All Bible quotations are from The Revised English Bible © Oxford University
Press and Cambridge University Press, 1989.

Cover design and photo by John Murello.

Printed in Canada.

1 2 3 4 5 6 7 8 9

Acknowledgments

Many of these essays first appeared in *Faith Alive*, a special feature of Catholic News Service. *Faith Alive* is a distinctive resource for stimulating reflection on matters of faith and the spiritual life. I am grateful to David Gibson and Carole Norris Greene, *Faith Alive* editors, for our ongoing relationship. It is a privilege to write for them.

I want to thank Emilie Cerar Mackney of Resurrection Press for her interest in and patience with this project. It is evident that she sees publishing as an instrument of evangelization. Her vision generates both hope and encouragement.

Once again, Bonnie Teresa Stallings provided technical expertise, a gift for which I am *always* grateful.

Contents

Part 3

The Communion of Saints (and Angels)

Part 4

The Challenge of Change

Foreword

In Psalm 46 we read: *"Be still and know that I am God"* *(46:10)*. Certain writers assist us both in reaching that inner stillness as well as opening the door to the mystery of God. Anne Morrow Lindbergh's *Gift from the Sea*, Thomas Merton's *Contemplative Prayer*, Henri Nouwen's *Reaching Out*, Kathleen Norris' *The Cloister Walk* are but a few examples of spiritual guides who point us in the direction of transcendence. We are indebted to them for helping us see that thousands of blessings surround us.

Dolores Leckey has practiced stillness and has been on a faith journey in pursuit of the mystery of God. As wife and mother, she knows the challenges of everyday spirituality. As a professional in Church work and as a writer, she is aware of the tensions that can upset the delicate balance between action and contemplation, between a busy apostolic life and the need for inner silence so essential for a creative life. As a pilgrim and sojourner, Dolores Leckey experiences the hungers of the heart — the hunger for meaning, the hunger for depth, the hunger for love.

In previous works Dolores has proven her ability as a perceptive writer and as an apt mentor. Her biography on the poet Jessica Powers — *Winter Music* — traced the history of a Wisconsin Carmelite poet and provided a helpful context in interpreting poems that arose out of silence and turned the mind and heart to God. In 1991, she published *Women and Creativity* (Paulist Press) and informed us that ". . .creativity requires a kind of disobedience to normality." A happy disobedience which she suffered and from which we gained.

Now, we are given yet another creative gem inviting us "to pause and take note" of all the blessings around us. To do that we are assisted by hearing the blessings in her life, blessings apprehended by noting the presence of God, blessings that arise when we gather with family and friends, blessings as we ponder the witnesses of faith who have gone before us, blessings that reside in the complex issue of our own times. In all of this we are shown the bounty of God, our extravagant, tremendous Lover. The underlying song through all the essays is the hymn of gratitude.

In *Blessings All Around Us* the reader will be challenged to pray and ponder the scriptures, to reflect on the contributions of such people as Brother Roger of Taizé, Catherine of Genoa, John Courtney Murray, to experience the beauty of leisure and the significance of family and friends, to wrestle with questions of surrender, aging, equality and conversion. A rich fare here. Much more than a cup of chicken soup — a hearty broth that sustains us for many miles.

Ralph Waldo Emerson comments: "All writing comes by the grace of God, and all doing and having." Dolores Leckey knows that. This slim, potent volume records the graced "doings and havings" of life; this substantive book is the result of a person writing out of an awareness that all is gift, all is grace, especially the gift of writing.

MOST REVEREND ROBERT F. MORNEAU
Auxiliary Bishop of Green Bay, Wisconsin
Author, Spiritual Director, Retreat Leader

Introduction

This is a book about the many dimensions of blessedness, the ways in which God's care touches and embraces us as we — ordinary people — make our way through life. The format is simple: a collection of short, reflective essays that invite the reader to pause and take note of *his or her* own blessings.

Long ago a wise monk advised me to incorporate some quiet, reflective time into each day when I would review the day's graces and the lapses from grace. In that way, he said, I would be in touch with the richness of my own life — the gifts of God — and the prodding of the Spirit to put faith into action. Without the reflective pause, he cautioned, it would be more difficult to grow in consciousness about God's hopes for me — and for the world — and whether or not I was helping or hindering their realization.

Daily pauses at first may seem impossible, although the most difficult part is simply to begin. However, an alternative method may be in order. Regular, focused, prayerful reflection, perhaps weekly (or even monthly), can certainly chart the way to a deeper awareness of God's blessed largesse. The goal is to become more attentive to our own experience wherein signs of God abound. *Blessings All Around Us* is conceived as a resource for doing that.

The essays are organized into four sections. The first is *The Presence of God*, which is about prayer, meditation, and the cultivation of our interior landscapes. This is followed by a section on *Ordinary Time and Holidays* where the presence of God in the company of others — community — is the subject for reflection. Section three is devoted to another aspect of community, what Catholic Christians refer to as *The Communion of Saints,* namely those who have gone before us into the full blessedness of life eternal. The saints offer us inspiration and practical guidance on how to live faithfully in the Holy Spirit. I have enlarged the scope of this term to include those other blessed beings we call angels, and the unnamed saints whom we celebrate on the feast of All Saints, November 1st. The fourth and final section, *The Challenge of Change* focuses on contemporary issues which require attentive, intelligent, and responsible decisions. All of us are faced with the application of what we have learned, from Church teaching and from our own explorations into the spiritual life, to the large and small issues and concerns that arise in our families, our parishes, our neighborhoods and in the larger society. The American bishops pointed out in *Called and Gifted for the Third Millennium* "while spirituality is more and more an explicit aspect of Christian life, 'spiritual sight' or insight is not sufficient in itself. The call to holiness requires effort and commitment to live the beatitudes."

Much of what I have learned about the bounty of God has come from the stories that men and women in all walks of life, from all parts of the world, have shared with me. In addition to my suggestions for *Ways to Ponder Your Blessings,* I invite you the reader to pause, listen to the inner word, remember the past, and imagine the future — and create your own reflective essays. You may prefer to "speak" your reflections, perhaps shared in your small faith communities, or to write them out. Whatever the form, I would appreciate learning about the blessings in your life. You may write me in care of Resurrection Press.

Part 1
The Presence of God

*Prayer is a right understanding of that
fullness of joy that is to come, along with
true longing and absolute trust that
we shall savor and see the bliss
that we are ordained to. . .*

*Prayer is a witness that the soul wills as
God wills.*

JULIAN OF NORWICH

- Recognizing God's Presence
- The Art of Listening...for God's Will
- Experiments in Prayer
- Looking at Jesus
- Understanding and Praying the Scriptures
- Prayer without End

Recognizing God's Presence

Winter was in the air at Holy Cross Abbey in Virginia when I began a weekend retreat there. Bare trees stood like sketches against the sky. The colors of winter filled the hillsides: burnt orange, a kind of gray rose, wisps of purple, bits of red berries here and there. A crisp slice of moon hinted at ice and snow. Silence was in the air.

Sometimes, it seems to me, a person needs to step back from the flow of ordinary life to see the treasures embedded in the rhythm of the days and nights. A retreat can provide such a respite — enabling one to see with fresh vision what always is present in life.

Retreats at Holy Cross, a Trappist abbey with a guest house, are simple and largely unstructured. During the course of several days one may attend the monks' chanting of the Divine Office and be present at Eucharist. Meals are taken in common with the other retreatants, but silently. The guestmaster may read or play music. Brother Steven chose to read from Loren Eiseley's *The Immense*

Journey, my husband's favorite book. Brother Steven considers Eiseley an example of a non-explicitly religious person who searched unceasingly for the face of God. Eiseley poked around in winter fields no longer lush with greenery, and studied buried roots and dying vegetation for clues to life's ultimate meaning.

As our weekend at Holy Cross unfolded I began to notice what I so often miss, and why. Hurry is one reason. The abbey's pace is totally unhurried. Everything in the monks' public life is done slowly and deliberately. The prayers are said aloud in half-note time, with the effect that each word has an appropriate gravity. Each word holds steady, echoes; each is "the word."

The first morning I thought about how much I needed to slow down and recognize, finally, that one of my defenses against God, against coming "near to the Face" (to use Brother Steven's phrase), is to be very busy, piling up deeds to accomplish, erecting a huge barricade. I saw that in the hurry, I miss the subtleties and details of life.

Crowded space is another block for me in seeing the details of my life — and finding God in them. The retreat, on the other hand, was an experience of spaciousness. The retreatants' rooms are ample; windows look out onto the spacious Virginia countryside.

The chapel, too, has an air of openness, yet everything and everyone seems well placed. The people are not overly separated from the monks, but separated enough. Visually speaking, we were part of the prayer, which in this space is to feel as if one is at the window looking out and looking in at the same time. Everything serves as a sign of God.

The silence of the monastery and of the retreat itself

reveals the extent to which noise (even pleasant noise) obliterates the still, small voice of God. A sign in the guest house reads: "Less is more." I know that to be true in many ways. There is a quality to the silence, a texture made rich through years, months, days, hours of prayer.

Prayer hangs in silence. And so one comes on retreat without any need to worry about how much one prays because simply being there is to be "in" the prayer that permeates everything. The silence is pure gift. In the silence every sound can be heard distinctly. Sometimes the sound is jarring. Sometimes it is like music. But out of the silence every sound comes forth alive. This was particularly noticeable when the psalms were sung. One surprising effect of the silence is the rest it provides. I was not aware I was so tired, but in the silence I slept easily and deeply. Brother Steven believes we rarely know how tired we really are. God knows, though, and silence is a way of divine soothing.

The presence of God in the Scriptures seems to have more shape, more intimacy because the word is spoken or sung in the monastery. The monastic melodies, ancient yet new, and so simple, rivet the attention. Each morning the cantor seemed to gather a great rush of energy to lead the final psalm. The result was a feeling of being sent forth into a new day. Since the retreat, rather than reading a psalm each morning, I've been saying it aloud, now and then trying a bit of a chant as well. Am I imagining that the words have more substance when released through song or speech?

It was Advent when I made that retreat. In the retreat's final hours I looked at the abbey's Advent wreath and saw in its candles new light to illuminate what it is that helps a person recognize God's daily presence. Along with uncluttered spaciousness, one profits from slowing down and enjoying the silence. Singing helps, too.

Ways to Ponder Your Blessings

1. Go back to a time that enabled you to step back from ordinary life and see with fresh vision. Is it time to plan for another "retreat"?

2. Where do you find "clues to life's ultimate meaning," and how do you incorporate them into your lifestyle?

3. If silence is a way of divine soothing, how can you create more opportunities for it daily? weekly? annually?

⤜❧ 2 ❧⤛

The Art of Listening...
for God's Will

A friend once said to me that the most problematic line in the Lord's Prayer is "Thy will be done." He went on to explain that while Christians repeat those words very frequently — daily even — he doubted if they really meant them. He had become aware that for him those words of Jesus could be translated as something like "Help me, God, to achieve *my* will." He believes he's not alone.

How often do we approach God with a question or a problem, already sure of the answer, wanting simply confirmation, and if possible, a little action? When we do, we may be short circuiting the Spirit's inspiration. How can we open ourselves in a more authentic way to God's guidance and influence — to live more fully, day by day, in the Spirit of God?

Scripture is our first and truest reference in this matter. In the First Book of Kings we learn that the voice of God is immersed in silence. Elijah discovers that neither the mighty wind, nor the fearful earthquake, nor the consuming fire revealed the Lord God. No. Elijah encountered the Holy One in a low, murmuring sound which some translations describe as sheer silence. Whether the encounter was one of silence or soft murmuring there is agreement that the noise and glitter — the grand gesture — were empty of the divine presence. God's abode was stillness.

The last years of this century and millennium are saturated with noise, from walkmen to "talk radio." I think we need to be intentional about silence, in some form, each day if possible, so that God's whispers are not buried in the extraneous "stuff" of contemporary society.

Early morning is my quiet time and space. Others find that ten or fifteen minutes after Mass cultivates silence. Many parishes are promoting a time of eucharistic adoration, and the habit of silence is developing that way. Deliberate "tuning out" of media can also help. Last Lent, for example, my husband and I tried a media fast at home in the "before work" morning hours. We found it so refreshing that it is now part of our household routine.

Cloistered nuns and monks who live immersed in silence have much to teach us. As one nun explained, "As you live the life. . .the silence just becomes as necessary and desirable as the air that you breathe every day."

Scripture also instructs us about the relationship between forgiveness and prayer. While faith is always emphasized in prayer matters, in the gospel of Mark the importance of forgiveness is added. "And when you stand praying, if you have a grievance against anyone, forgive him, so that your Father in heaven may forgive you the wrongs you have done" (Mk 11:25). It is possible to block the pathways to God's Holy Spirit with an accumulation of hurts, vengeful thoughts, harsh judgments and "wishing evil," disguised though they may be. This inner debris needs to be recognized, confessed and let go.

With the practice of silence, and the clearing of our inner space, our prayer may very well be reshaped. Rather than praying for the ratification of our own solutions we are likely to ask genuine, open-ended questions of God. "What do you want me to do Lord?" may yield something like, "Do nothing." That requires courage for an activist like me. It seems like God's will may be that I join in the divine waiting for the time being.

Or the small, still whisper which responds to concern for a lonely family member may be directing me to some simple action: a letter, a visit, a phone call. No grand gestures here, only ordinary, compassionate reaching out.

A spiritual community of some kind is helpful for testing the insights heard in prayer. A wise spiritual director can help test the promptings, placing them in the context of Catholic spiritual theology and practice. A prayer group or intentional small Christian community can also help us to see where precisely God is drawing us, and how that fits into the larger context of our vocations.

Evelyn Underhill, one of the great spiritual writers of this century, wrote that our prayer must have no craving, clutching or clinging, all of which speak of willfulness. Rather, we are to enter into a state of willingness: to be, to act, to endure. The willingness makes all the difference; it leads into the region of God's will.

To be women and men of prayer — to live with the Spirit — means:

> . . . to be a listener.
> It is to keep the vigil of mystery,
> earthless and still.

One leans to catch the stirring of the Spirit,
strange as the wind's will.
. . . [And,] To live with the Spirit of God
is to be a lover.

To Live with the Spirit

These lines, taken from a poem by Carmelite poet Jessica Powers, give wise guidance for prayer. To truly listen we have to move out of our set ways; we must "lean." And we must love. For finally, prayer without love is no prayer at all.

Ways to Ponder Your Blessings

1. How can I begin to be "intentional about silence"?

2. What will your prayer look like if it is "to have no craving, clutching or clinging"?

3. Describe a time when "(you leaned) to catch the stirring of the Spirit."

Experiments in Prayer

*T*he critical first step into the mysteries of prayer is simply to begin.

Imagine waking in the morning, making a cup of coffee, sitting in a comfortable, supportive chair, closing your eyes, taking a deep breath and acknowledging God's presence. When you move beyond imagining, and actually clear some time and space for this encounter, you have begun to pray.

These early prayer times may be brief, five to fifteen minutes, but no matter. Faithful presence is what counts!

So does authenticity. Wise spiritual directors remind us to pray as we can, not as we can't.

When we come to pray, we may be grieving over some desperate loss or rejoicing over good fortune. We may feel confused or empty. Whatever our present condition, that is the place to start. For one aspect of prayer is laying before God the truth of our lives, presenting our real selves.

If we listen as well as talk when we pray, we are likely

to hear the human needs that touch and sometimes break the heart of Christ. These concerns may be as close as our children or as far away as the world's refugees.

As we listen we are directed to join our will to God's will by acting out the Beatitudes in contemporary settings: comforting, making peace, seeking justice, simplifying our lives.

One way to develop our listening power in prayer is to use the Scriptures. A Gospel passage, a psalm, or one of the soaring passages from Paul's letters can serve as a point of departure for our dialogue with the Spirit.

Psalm 90 says that "seventy is the sum of years, or eighty, if we are strong." That phrase always claims my attention and leads me to pray that I won't squander whatever future remains for me and that I will choose my priorities in light of life's limits.

If I listen, I may hear God's suggestions to do less, savor more and measure everything in terms of love.

The next step is to act upon the insight gained in prayer. I may hesitate or stumble, but this action step is critical. It closes the circle of prayer.

Often an action that flows from prayer is more prayer for people and events.

Over the years as I prayed for my children growing into adulthood, I discovered the power in the action of holding these free, unique, men and women in God's light, the light of Pentecost. This relieved me from figuring out precisely what my grown children should do. Rather, my love for them could be joined with God's, trusting that the Spirit would know what paths they should follow.

Time after time I watched them follow the light; time after time I thanked God for saving me from my penchant to control the drama of life unfolding in them.

People who like to walk, by the way, can discover the joys of prayer-walking. Choose a Scripture verse, and ponder that inspired word with every step. Or imagine walking with Jesus, much as his friends did in Galilee's meadows.

Ask for guidance and blessing. Listen carefully for Christ's word. It will come.

Not all prayer is solitary. Often joining others makes us conscious of the holy presence. Even with busy schedules families still gather for meals, and that time can draw people into prayer.

In our family we have tended to say a standard grace learned in childhood. On great feasts we sing the doxology. But lately on the rare occasions when grown children from afar gather, along with a grandchild or two, we ask someone to pray from the heart.

One evening, 11-year-old Sam, who had visited museums with his grandfather all day, prayed for the hungry children in the world saying, "I hope no one will ever be as hungry as I was today." That's when we realized grandfather and Sam had forgotten lunch!

As small Christian communities grow within the church, men and women experience the power of prayer together. Sometimes their prayer asks God to aid families, parishes, neighborhoods. Sometimes prayer leads the small community to some form of mission.

One group I know began an affordable housing project, an outgrowth of study and prayer together. Another group supported a member in her election to the school board. Yet another began a support system for immigrants. None of these initiatives would have happened without prayer.

Someone once gave me a book called *Prayer Can Change Your Life.* I've forgotten much of its contents, but the title remains with me.

From the beginning of the Christian era when the apostles and a group of women, including Jesus' mother, were gathered in the Upper Room and enveloped by the Holy Spirit, prayer has ignited the divine spark in people. The world of the Galileans was about to expand beyond anything they could imagine. And so it goes, from generation to generation.

Prayer — however brief, however simple, however silent — changes everything, most especially the pray-er.

Ways to Ponder Your Blessings

1. How is prayer a mystery?

2. In what way has prayer changed your life?

ं 4 ं

Looking at Jesus

*A*nyone who has practiced the *Spiritual Exercises of St. Ignatius* knows how important the imagination is in that form of prayer. The retreatant is asked to enter into the Gospel scene, visualizing the first century Mediterranean culture: the sights, sounds, smells. One might envision the fields of Galilee ablaze with poppies, a usual sight in that part of the world. Or one might feel the exciting pulse of busy Jerusalem. The women of Bethany. . . Peter. . . the boy with barley bread — all are part of the visualization. And the pray-er is encouraged to see Jesus in his home-land, with friends (and enemies), with the people of that time, place, and culture. The pray-er is also encouraged to interact with Jesus. St. Teresa of Avila favored this form of prayer, probably learned from Jesuit advisors.

The Jesus encountered in this scriptural prayer is dynamic. I see him astonished as the paralytic man is low-ered through the roof of the house where he is teaching. Other times he seems deeply moved by the woman who washes his feet with her tears. (Do his tears mingle with hers, I wonder?) Often, I see him striding purposefully toward Bethany where hospitality awaits or toward Jerusalem where tragedy hides. I tag along, with questions or requests, seeking guidance and courage. Usually, I'm out of breath.

What does he look like? The great Russian icongrapher Andrei Rublev has given me Jesus' face, the one I see most often in these meditations: all of humanity is there, all of it; and all of God is there. The eyes are key. Jesus' eyes see through me — and everyone — to the heart of the matter. He's reading the human heart, with all its complexity and mixed signals. This is the Jesus I rely on.

Always he is reading the human situation with a depth of understanding. He knows that people make a mess of things, but that the mercy of God reaches into the mess, and transforms it. I see Rublev's Jesus as he tells the story of the self-righteous religious official (the Pharisee) and the public sinner (the tax collector). The Pharisee expresses gratitude that he is not like the rest of humanity — greedy, dishonest, adulterous–and he reminds God that he is rigorous in his religious practices of fasting and alms-giving. Meanwhile the tax-collector, all too aware of his human failings, simply prays for God's mercy. One gets the feeling that Jesus doesn't have too much patience with religious arrogance.

More than anything I think Jesus deals with the essence of life, not the accidentals. He tries to convince the Samaritan woman that the true worship of God is a spiritual matter, not dependent on a particular mountain or even a particular temple. Over and over again, I see Jesus calling people into a sense of personal responsibility. He enlivens their freedom with the example of his own. On the Sabbath he cures the ill (Luke 13, e.g.); he defends his disciples who, hungry, pick corn on the Sabbath (Mark 2). He tries to awaken the people of that time and ours to the centrality of human need in the web of religious regulation.

The Jesus I meet in these meditations honors the human condition. He weeps (for his friend, for his city); he laughs and celebrates (at weddings and dinners); he draws people into the center of their own souls, constantly asking them to name their desires. He loves his friends and forgives them their betrayals. You see it all in the eyes of Rublev's icon. I think poet Jessica Powers saw those eyes:

> I never try to probe the sky's blue span;
> I never look too deep into the sea
> But the dim face of a tragedian
> looks out at me.
>
> Neither the night nor day can find a place
> where I have not been shaken with surprise
> at the white beauty of a holy face
> and two great lonely eyes.
>
> *The Mystic Face*

All through the Gospel, Jesus' eyes are telling his story. He raises his eyes and notices a large crowd coming toward him. They must be hungry, he says, so he feeds them. He's approached by a rich young man who wants to join the followers of Jesus, but he can't let go of his securities. Jesus looks at him with love, we read, as the young man goes his own way (Luke 10). Hours before his death he raises his eyes to heaven in prayer, in prayer for those who are his own (John 17).

It is said that the eyes are the windows of the soul. With a great and holy icon (like Rublev's) the eyes are said to see into the heart and soul of the beholder. And so, with Jesus, living in scripture, in the sacraments, in one another. He looks at us all with love, understanding our great need for mercy, helping us to see the way things really are.

Ways to Ponder Your Blessings

1. Using your imagination, pray today's Gospel reading interacting with the people in it. Use your journal to record your experience.

2. Use a crucifix, holy card or Rublev's icon of Jesus to initiate your prayer time today.

ᘓᕩᔓ 5 ᘓᕩᔓ

Understanding and Praying
the Scriptures

I am forever indebted to the Benedictines for handing on
the tradition of *lectio divina*. In this form of prayer, one
chooses a passage of scripture, reads it through, and then
reads again, slowly and attentively, stopping when a word
seems to arrest attention. There is the sense that the scripture passage — the living word of God — has initiated a
conversation. One may dwell on the word, ponder it, follow it through paths of insight and inspiration. One may
rest deeply with it. Countless generations have grown in
the ways of biblical prayer by practicing *lectio*.

I am grateful, also, to the Jesuits for preserving and
teaching St. Ignatius' imaginative way of scriptural prayer
where we experience an inner encounter with Jesus. Both
these forms of scriptural meditation and prayer are cher-
ished by people all over the world.

And then along come the Scripture scholars, linguistic
and literary experts, archaeologists and geographers, cultural anthropologists and historians who offer facts to

complement devotion. Do they help or hinder our prayer? I think they help, enriching the imagination and deepening the conversation of *lectio divina* or Ignatian meditation. Take the parables. When we can situate them in the context of first century Jewish culture we can see how utterly radical Jesus' teaching was.

In the Prodigal Son story the father simply does not fit the image of a village patriarch of that particular time and culture. He's not interested in dispensing justice to his wastrel younger son who returns home only when he is totally down and out. No. He's more interested in celebrating the joy he feels at seeing his son again. He treats the wastrel as if nothing terrible or insulting had happened! And those of us who think of strict justice as the bottom line may not understand this response, and probably don't like it.

Or take the story of the Good Shepherd. When we know something about the ways of sheep-tending in the first century we realize that a "normal" shepherd would not go in search of one lost sheep and leave the rest of the flock to fend for themselves — not to mention the danger to the shepherd on craggy precipices. But the Good Shepherd has different standards, and there is no boundary on the costly love required to find the lost one.

These and other parables about "finding the lost" redefine the conventional meaning of love. So when we get to the Letters of John we understand a little better his radical definition of God, namely love without limits, *agapic* love. A natural next step is to look for that love in our own surroundings, to glimpse the God who is passing by.

Today the Lord can be seen where parents lovingly care for a son dying of AIDS. Or with a couple in mid-life who have raised a family but who adopt a small child that no one wants. We know the Lord is passing by when a Bosnian Serb shelters a Croat or a Muslim — or the Croat or Muslim does likewise. Becoming familiar with the culture of the scriptures helps us to interpret biblical love in our own cultural context.

So does history. Imagine journeying through Israel immersed in Josephus' *History of the Jewish Wars* which describes in gory detail the historical period in which Jesus was born. I did, and as I read about the thousands of Jews slaughtered because they would not bend to Roman authority, or because they would not permit defilement of the temple, I grasped something of the determination of the race from which Jesus sprang, as well as the turmoil and turbulence of his times. This knowledge makes his message of forgiveness, reconciliation and peace seem even more of a counterpoint.

The archaeologists unearth the artifacts of culture, and give us bits and pieces of daily life in Galilee, bringing Peter and John — and Jesus — more vividly to our imaginations.

Scripture scholars unravel the Greek of the original texts, and new interpretations and new levels of meaning emerge. They tell us, for example, that in Matthew's gospel "seeking the kingdom of God" and seeking justice are not two distinct quests. Clearly, this kind of knowledge can shape our intent as we pray, "Thy kingdom come."

Like many people I have a particular prayer space at home. The bible is there, but so is the *Rule of Benedict* and the *Spiritual Exercises of St. Ignatius.* And I'm happy to say *The New Jerome Biblical Commentary* has recently joined these old favorites. Together they offer endless adventures of the mind, the heart and the spirit.

Ways to Ponder Your Blessings

1. Using the method of *lectio divina* pray today's Gospel or your favorite Scripture selection.

2. In addition to her bible, the author also keeps copies of *The Rule of Benedict, The Spiritual Exercises of St. Ignatius* and *The Jerome Biblical Commentary* in her prayer corner. Which of these or others do you find worthwhile for prayer?

❧ 6 ❧

Prayer without End

*M*any people find the Letters of Paul an easy spring-board into prayer. That may be because the Letters themselves are filled with the writer's own heartfelt prayer for his readers, not unlike the heart-prayers of many a parent.

We may use different words, but do not mothers and fathers the world over beseech God for their children of all ages: "That you may receive from him all wisdom and spiritual understanding for full insight into his will" (Col 1:9-10). They pray for these insights and for virtue not only for their children but as importantly, for themselves.

Prayer in families is often hidden but I submit it is ceaseless:

- Parents trying to care for a newborn, mentally form little prayers asking for guidance, wisdom, rest.
- A single mother, seemingly stretched beyond her physical and emotional boundaries, prays for wisdom to understand what is going on with her child who may be sad, angry, or confused. Alone, without the child's father to contribute to the pool of wis-

dom, she has only God for sustenance. In the silence of the night she waits for the still, small voice that confronted Elijah on Mt. Horeb.

- A family suddenly finds that the grandparents, who were always available for counsel or just fun, are now fragile and ill — so suddenly it seems — that only prayer can help them adjust to the new and permanent situation. Teenagers and their parents are joined in recitation of the rosary for their dearly loved and now needy elders.

All of these situations reflect family prayer, which sometimes we associate only with group prayer, like parents and children together reciting the rosary which has of course been a favorite form of family prayer. But we are not limited to this "group experience" or to any one kind of group experience.

A young man I know, married and expecting his first child, stopped by his parents' apartment one spring evening to say a final good-bye to them. He was en route to Moscow for three months of necessary research. His wife, also a graduate student, expecting their first child, was unable to accompany him to Russia. The young people were experiencing a certain amount of sadness and stress. The small ecclesial community to which the parents belonged — a community of study, prayer and corporate action — was meeting at his parents' apartment when he came for the farewell. After a cup of coffee, some conversation, some handshakes and hugs, the young couple were ready to depart. Suddenly a man in the group said, "Wait a minute! We can't let him go without a prayer." A circle formed and each one prayed for the young man, for his wife, his child, his work. He in turn uttered words of thanksgiving for this extended family who had known him since childhood, put up with his antics, and remained interested in the direction of his life. "We pray that you may bear fruit in active goodness of every kind, and grow in the knowledge of God" (Col 1: 10). Not just knowledge of Russian manuscripts, dear son, but the knowledge of God.

Evelyn Underhill, the 20th century English writer on the spiritual and mystical life, claimed that the little wayside shrines and chapels that dotted the pilgrimage route to Canterbury had the texture of prayer in them. By that she meant that centuries of people stopping to pray in those places had created a palpable sense of faith and love and hope that still greeted one today.

The same kind of thing can be said about a home. The fact of prayer creates an atmosphere. Of what? Of love, first of all. Parents who pray for their children, for each other, for the world given unto their care, shape the home environment as surely as flowers and photos and paintings do. One enters such a home and meets a spiritual presence invited through prayers of praise and pleading, of gratitude and repentance. This is not to say that trouble is absent from such places. But it is to say that trouble is engaged not denied. Years ago a friend told me how she felt the power of her prayer for her twelve-year-old son who was showing signs of mild depression. For weeks she had been praying for him "to come out of it." One day she prayed that she would do whatever was necessary — even family counseling to which she felt some resistance — to help her son. The prayer was from the deepest part of her conscious being. She knew as soon as the prayer was formulated that help and guidance were on the way. (Counseling was not needed but for years she remained open to it, and to "whatever" would help her family.)

Peace was central in that family's home even when there were tears of sorrow or hurt. Love — God's love, our love — does such things.

As our prayer deepens and develops it spills out into other segments of human need; this happens because prayer and love are the same substance. They cannot remain bottled up.

These days many of us turn from the newscasts about Haiti or Rwanda or Kosovo toward the prayer of Paul:

> I kneel in prayer to the Father, from whom
> every family in heaven and on earth takes its name
> that out of the treasures of his glory he may
> grant you strength and power through his Spirit
> in your inner being, that through faith Christ
> may dwell in your hearts in love.
>
> *Eph 3:14-17*

We pray not only for our own families but for the shattered ones of those troubled lands. Perhaps we do well to recall my friend who said to God, "I will do whatever is necessary."

That is the border of prayer and action; the step from *my* family to the family of God.

Ways to Ponder Your Blessings

1. What has been your experience of family prayer?

2. How have you felt the power of prayer for your family, friends, community?

Part 2
Ordinary Time and Holidays

"*Take the present situation as it is and try to deal with what it brings you, in a spirit of generosity and love. God is as much in the difficult home problems as in the times of quiet and prayer.*"

LETTERS, EVELYN UNDERHILL

"*In the house of God there is never-ending festival; the angel choir makes eternal holiday; the presence of God's face gives joy that never fails.*"

ST. AUGUSTINE, ON PSALM 41

- The Culture of Life: Attention and Risk
- Places of Grace
- Children's Truth
- Family Intimacy
- Discovering Holidays
- Advent Inspirations
- Christmas Light

⚜ 7 ⚜

The Culture of Life:
Attention and Risk

*I*n *Follow the Way of Love*, the bishops of the United States speak of the family as a wellspring of life. They refer, of course, to the foundational creative act of bringing a child into the world, or of welcoming a child by adoption into the family. But they also had in mind the perduring tasks of nurturing children into their adult lives of responsibility and service.

Christian life is not simply focused on the nuclear family; the arc of concern reaches far and wide. Neighborhood children, other parents, networks of relatives and friends–all need the love and support and attention that makes life flourish. Christian life, modeled on the Trinity, is ultimately about community where the giftedness of the members is exercised for the common good. Again, the bishops phrase it this way: "Each generation of a family is challenged to leave the world a more beautiful and beneficial place than it inherited." This might mean bringing a meal to a sick neighbor, helping to build or find homes for poor people, recycling your goods, becoming politically active, reading poetry instead of diatribes against public officials.

Recently, with the Church's entrance into "ordinary time" I found myself remembering about two "extraordinary events" of the past; a Christmas season and the blizzard of 1996, and the various expressions of life at those times.

Our adult children live in different parts of the country, some with young families of their own. Christmas visits are sometimes brief and staggered. Several years ago however, everyone gathered for a New Year's Eve dinner. In between bites of saffron rice and sips of red wine, one baby was being nursed, another was trying to navigate a staircase. The new parents were totally attentive as if their baby was the first on earth. I watched as every baby need was anticipated, realizing that loving concentration made it possible.

When the babies finally slept, our dessert conversation turned to the year just ended. The birth of Monica a month before was at the top of everyone's "most important events" list. After that items varied. My husband said getting to know the homeless people in the shelter where he volunteers introduced him to new dimensions of resilience and trust. He's amazed at how people manage their lives even when they have nothing.

Our daughter shared that visiting the Vermeer exhibit at the National Gallery of Art was a spiritual experience. She waited several hours on a long, cold line and declared the wait worthwhile. Each painting has a soul, she said, and she wept as she moved from one to another.

Mary Kate, actress turned nurse, said that caring for sick children (a completely new experience) taught her volumes about straightforward courage.

The evening took on a tone of gratitude.

Eventually the young families went home: to Pittsburgh, to New York City, to California. The Christmas tree was barely down when the blizzard came. As grocery store lines sometimes extended outside, newspapers and mail remained undelivered, and residential streets were unplowed, people seemed isolated by more than snow. Habits of individualism held sway. Except here and there. One story, in particular, showed me how one small risk can spark a spirit of community.

A colleague told me how she and her husband experienced the culture of life in the midst of snow, ice and fatigue. She lives at the bottom of a hill which comes to a dead end at some woods. For four days no city plows or salt trucks visited that hidden cul-de-sac. Vehicles, even four-wheel drives, could not get out of the mountains of snow. Her anxiety level rose rapidly when she heard a second storm was approaching; she felt she had to get to work in Washington, D.C. Her husband, Andre, decided to try to dig them out.

My friend joined her husband and together they cleared their driveway, a neighbor's driveway and the street in front. Two neighbors further up the street, working on their sidewalks, stopped and stared at the street-clearing effort. Before long they, too, were clearing a piece of the street.

As the small snow crew made their way up the street, Andre took a deep breath, and began knocking on doors, asking people to come out and help. He had no idea what their response would be.

One by one, they ventured forth: the grandson of a neighbor, an older gentleman, six younger men and one woman. As they worked they told each other their names (some for the first time); they talked about the local government and who knows what else. As they realized that they were actually going to clear the whole street they became excited and even exhilarated. Though tired, some began the mammoth job of digging out their cars.

When it was all over — eight hours later — everyone said how good they felt about the joint effort. The joy was contagious. Women, who earlier had trudged through knee-high snow to get provisions from a local store, came home to a cleared street, their faces full of smiles. Some of them joined the shovelers, eager to be part of the newly formed community, which was, in effect, liberating the residents there. People could now go to work, shop, catch the bus at the top of the hill. They could check on the elderly with greater ease. And if an emergency vehicle was needed, it could get to its destination. All this because Andre risked getting doors slammed in his face.

Life doesn't just happen. It takes risks, attention and communication to foster a culture of life. The results are often surprising.

Ways to Ponder Your Blessings

1. On what occasions has your family been "a well-spring of life"?

2. Describe a time when you liberated or were liberated by the actions of others.

❦ 8 ❦

Places of Grace

One of the great discoveries of marriage and family life is that God's presence — sacred mystery — emerges in the ordinariness of it all. We need not travel great distances in arduous pilgrimage to reach a divine threshold. The threshold is amazingly near, through the doorways of our homes — the domestic church — and through the doorways of our parish church — home to gathered families. Memories of each of these "homes," echoes of one another, can infuse the measure of our days with meaning and purpose. How?

First there is the welcome. Our family, influenced perhaps by the *Rule of Benedict* (as apt for families as for monks) rejoices in guests. We like to cook; we like to gather around the table; we like to talk, especially about politics and history, which inevitably includes religion and family stories. We remember these times as Christ moments.

Sunday worship in our parish enlarges our experience of hospitality. Founded as an African-American mission parish in the early part of this century, people from varied ethnic backgrounds now gather on Sunday morning. The richness of the world church is evident each Sunday as together we listen to the stories of Jesus, his disciples, and the Church's beginnings, all woven together with contemporary issues. When our pastor preaches, he is as likely to include elements of immigration law, recent newspaper editorials, and local needs, as he is patristics and theology. This "church family" continues the conversation initiated at Mass over breakfast in the parish hall where newcomers are invited into the ever-widening conversation. Words of liturgy and words of family meld into a consciousness of Christ beckoning to us to keep enlarging the circle of concern.

So much of what occurs within the walls of our small church building, the gestures and the words of Sunday liturgy, resonate with life outside those walls.

We pray for those near, (the sick and the "homeless and homebound" prays one woman each Sunday.) And we pray for those who are far away. At Mass, it is the Haitians and the Salvadorans. At home, I think of our new Palestinian and Jewish friends whom we met in Israel, as my husband and I recite Psalm 122 in the evening: "Pray for the peace of Jerusalem/May those who love you prosper."

At Mass the priest offers bread and wine to God the Father calling it the work of our hands. This offering reminds me of Margaret who brings me vegetables and flowers from the garden plot she cultivates so tenderly. What of the work of my hands, I wonder? Do words and documents nourish anyone; or provide beauty?

As consecrated bread is broken — Christ's very self — I see the brokenness of our congregation:

My dear friends who have ended a thirty-year marriage unleashing waves of sorrow within their community of friends and family.

Lamb of God, have mercy on them.

I notice the woman next to me whose son was killed in a drive-by shooting.

Lamb of God, mercy please.

Alcoholism. . .poor housing. . . unemployment. . . old people alone, isolated. . . violence in the home and in the heart, on the street. . .*Grant us peace.*

With communion, peace comes. Jenny offers me the bread of life, as she does to all who come forward. The suffering is made bearable, if only for a moment. She is as radiant now as she was decades ago when she led civil rights marches. These days she organizes volunteers for the soup kitchen and raises money for the youth group, and — thankfully — she decorates the church for weddings. Jenny is teaching us about graceful aging.

The *Catechism of the Catholic Church* states, "The Paschal Mystery of Christ. . . cannot remain only in the past. . . The event of the Cross and Resurrection abides and draws everything toward life" (#1085).

I not only believe that statement, I know it to be true. My family, our guests, my pastor, Jenny, my fellow parishioners engrave this truth upon my heart. The threshold of home and the threshold of Church are very close, indeed.

Ways to Ponder Your Blessings

1. Meditate on the words of the Mass: "work of our hands." How does the "work of your hands" bring life and hope?

2. Ponder this: "the event of the Cross and Resurection abides and draws everything toward life." How is this true for you?

⤔ 9 ⤔

Children's Truth

*P*sychiatrist Robert Coles is a close, caring observer of children and their inner world. He has spent countless hours with the children of the South before and during the years of the civil rights movement. It was he who gave us a glimpse into the soul of Ruby Bridges, the 6-year-old African-American girl who braved mobs to attend a newly desegregated school in New Orleans.

Coles told of a Federal Marshall, a former Marine, who said he never had seen such courage as Ruby's, even in war. One day he asked Ruby if she was scared. After all, she had to walk through a sea of violence and obscenities day after day. Ruby's reply was transparent in its simplicity:

"I just do what my granny says. I keep on praying."

Sometimes grandparents see and hear things in the new generation that were blurred when they were raising their own children.

One time I was driving along the New England Coast with my then 4-year-old grandson, Sam. Suddenly, night fell and with the dark, an all-encompassing fog.

I was unfamiliar with the road and did not know if it was safe to pull to the side. To me it seemed the most prudent course was to proceed slowly. "Say a prayer, Sam," I said almost automatically. Soon I heard a small confident voice praying, "O God, lift the fog that we may see."

Over and over Sam intoned his prayer. His mother, a linguistics teacher, was thrilled with her son's sentence structure. I was thrilled because it seemed God had guided a small boy into the realm of genuine prayer.

An 80-year-old nun I shared this episode with, added that Sam's prayer could be a daily prayer for most of us. There are many kinds of fog, she said.

Years ago when I read Carla Needleman's description of her work teaching a pottery student, I recognized parallels in the family. Ms. Needleman wrote: "While we were working together I felt how different we were and how locked each was in her own attitudes. . . Somehow she found her own quiet way of understanding what was needed. . . Perhaps after all there had been an unseen exchange of understanding between us, a magical osmosis through the tough membrane separating us. . . I probably will not be able to know if her experience with me and with the potter's wheel will affect her life outside the studio."

Something similar happens in a family. I help a child with homework, and at first he seems determined not to understand. If I stay with the perception, I leave him to his own devices or accuse him of being obstinate. Tears often follow.

But if I step back a bit and marvel at the difference in us, maybe I can wait with him a little longer until he finds his way into the work.

Another example: I decide to teach my child to set the table correctly. I can give him directions. Then I can leave, come back, correct his mistakes. Or I can "be" with him, giving him my time, my precious time, as he learns. In both instances, I might ask: Has my son learned more than mathematics or the art of table setting? Will my teaching affect his life outside the home? Maybe. Will it affect my life? Assuredly.

Something else in Ms. Needleman's reflections seems important: the image of the "tough membrane" that separated Needleman from her student. Children are not born with tough membranes separating them from the visible or invisible world.

Coles again has a telling story, this one about a 9-year-old boy in a wealthy community who went to church most Sundays. The boy listened carefully to sermons about Jesus and the poor. Then the boy began to dream about the poor and asked his parents to do something for people on the streets. His parents took him to the pastor, who told the boy not to take literally what he heard in church and recommended some counseling.

Coles used this true story to point out the many forms of deprivation children encounter. The boy's spiritual awareness was considered deviant.

One might assume that in due time the boy will learn how to remain unaffected by the sermons he hears. But I suspect his "checked" sensibilities will be surrounded by a sadness.

The most important task for any parent, grandparent, teacher or pastor is children's formation. This means, first, that adults have to be committed to their own ongoing formation. We can only give what we have.

A second factor is time: spending time with children. We need to listen to their imaginings — the stuff of children's inner lives.

We need to listen with understanding to their fears and dreams. We can pray with them, read or be silent with them, play with them.

Parents learn about themselves by watching and listening to their children. We see, as on a screen, our own fears, our petty behaviors. But we see our enlightened side, too: our generosity, creativity, compassion.

As reflectors of our way of being in the world, children can be the means for adult re-formation.

Ways to Ponder Your Blessings

1. Use Sam's prayer as a mantra today: "O God, lift the fog that we may see."

2. How have children been reflectors and a means for your re-formation?

❦ 10 ❦

Family Intimacy

*I*n the foyer of St. Mary's Seminary in Baltimore, Maryland, is a statue of Mary holding her child. I always am struck by the figures' warmth and intimacy. The mother cradles her child, her face touching his head.

I think even an alien from outer space would conclude from that statue that St. Mary's is a place of welcome and love — a nurturing place.

The statue expresses the earliest experience of intimate love, that of mother and child. There are qualities in this first love that we all long to return to in some way.

As small children, "we know our mother's affection before we can begin to understand it," writes Daniel Epstein in *Love's Compass.*

Epstein's abiding memory is one of his mother rocking him, the chair creaking familiarly. They seemed almost one body in their closeness.

The mother-child relationship is, in a way, an initiation into mystery. It touches something deep within, the place of our beginning, to paraphrase poet T.S. Eliot. I think this early closeness stirs some preconscious memory of our beginning place, the heart of God.

In time, the child experiences intimacy in the fuller family circle — what Epstein calls the "glorious pressure cooker" of family life among siblings.

We are thrust into intimate circumstances with brothers and sisters, and far into adulthood, siblings can call forth all kinds of passion from one another without effort.

Life among siblings is a unique form of intimacy, preparing us for the ever-widening circle of love as we move out to form deep friendships.

Childhood best friends share secrets and hopes, learning to trust each other and to tolerate each other's shortcomings.

With adolescence, the opposite sex moves to the center of interest. Still, girls at this point tend to have best friends with whom they talk for hours and share the heart's secrets. Frequently, boys opt for teams and a certain privacy about feelings.

Such patterns can show up later in a couple's different approaches to intimacy. These differences are frequently the reason married couples seek counseling.

Differences notwithstanding, marriage creates a unique intimacy both of best friends, as the partners work through communications differences, as well as of physical desire, knowledge and comfort.

And married people uniquely understand how conjugal love is about so much more than sexual passion. It involves connecting with one another when self-esteem is damaged, building bridges, forgiveness and reconciliation.

It is also about remembering. The tone and meaning of ordinary marital intimacy is caught in a novel by Robb Forman Dew titled *Dale Loves Sophie to Death*. The novel's married couple are separated over a summer. When reunited, they reconnect in the ordinariness of marital intimacy and their "instinctive inclination to turn toward the other." The author writes:

"Each one had expected that the other would be too tired to make love. In fact, they made love with a gentle and slow pleasure, because their energy was not great. Their passion was not ragged or insistent, and Dinah was glad that her body was allowing her this great enjoyment; she wasn't hindered by vanity and self-evaluation; she was not being judged."

The couple felt at ease at last, and "in the morning they were fond and affectionate with each other and with the children. Their physical isolation from the other had made them forget how to be familiar, and now they remembered."

Sexual love seems a valuable way to bridge inevitable estrangements in marriage which happen because of illness or travel or other obligations that remove one from the intimate rhythms of life, of home.

Rhythm is basic to intimacy. Closeness and oneness do not happen at a steady pace. Research indicates that marital intimacy, including sexual expression, and the sense of being emotionally and psychologically "in tune," are cyclical.

The cycle of marital intimacy consists of falling in love, settling into a routine, descending into a crisis and beginning again. The cycle repeats itself often, with varying degrees of intensity.

But people married a short time may assume the cycle's crisis part signals their basic incompatibility. Patience and time are needed to see the cycle through. Over the years, memory strengthens one in crisis times.

This is why it is important that long-married couples be available to counsel young married people, to remind them that a time to begin again is on the horizon.

People married many years sometimes speak of the depth of intimacy felt by simply being in the same house, though there may be little conversation. An intense awareness of the other develops bit by bit over the years. Epstein knew this. He writes: "In my grandmother's house there was a vibration. . . like the diminishing echo of a cello chord. The sound was unmistakable to a boy of 5. . . Not for another 20 years would I understand that the vibration in my grandparents' house was love."

That's it. The statue at St. Mary's Seminary echoes that vibration.

I can't help but wonder if all our loving acts, all our moments of intimacy, are readying us for the great angel chorus, the sounds of God and all God's people in love.

Ways to Ponder Your Blessings

1. Use a statue or holy card of Mary holding Jesus to initiate your prayer time today.

2. Think of a time you were separated from a loved one and what it felt like to be reunited.

❦ *11* ❦

Discovering Holidays

*L*eisure is essential to the "good life." However, true leisure is very hard for humans to enter. I've thought about leisure for decades. How many times have I vowed to establish the Aristotelian balance of work and leisure? And how often have the scales tipped in the direction of work? I've lost count.

I write under the influence of Josef Pieper as well as the memory of a recent summer vacation. Pieper's classic essay, "Leisure, the Basis of Culture," argues that leisure — not to be confused with laziness or inactivity — is essential to a fully human life. But Pieper tells us leisure is not simply a break in one's work life, whether for an hour, a day or a week. Leisure has more endurance than that, sharing qualities of contemplation and celebration. But not just ordinary celebration.

No. For Pieper the celebration must consist of the stuff of divine worship, where one experiences nothing less than the generosity of God. Make no mistake: For Pieper true leisure is not simply a means to an end, namely more and better work. His kind of leisure enables one to grasp the world as a whole and to enter into the festival of God's universe, what he called "an unending holiday."

With a spate of books now available about the American penchant for overworking and numerous surveys highlighting the wish of parents and children for more quality time, Pieper might yet rise from the ashes of the 1950s.

For me, even vacations once came cloaked in usefulness. One could read and write at the beach, improve the tennis game, teach the children to play bridge — all this bracketed with meals and laundry, definitely not what Pieper had in mind. Only prayer presented a different way.

So I gave up beach reading for looking: waves, birds, subtleties in sand, grasses. I began to walk and pray, enjoying other people's gardens. And then one summer my husband and I joined other walkers in the Cotswolds for what is called a Holiday Fellowship. Each day groups set out with a guide for three miles, seven miles or as much as ten. All day we were gone. We walked through pastures, woods and villages, pausing in churchyards for lunch and a bit of history. It was tiring but sweet. (Holiday Fellowship began at the turn of the century when an alert pastor, concerned for rural folk now transported to urban areas, established the walking holiday as an inexpensive, leisurely way of staying familiar with the soul of nature and the soul of humanity.) For two weeks that summer the world of accomplishments rested. Oh, we felt good about making a steep ascent or completing ten miles, but the real satisfaction came from connectedness. To appreciate our human connection to the whole universe, time spent "in" nature is important. We celebrated the terrain, the nesting birds, the unusual wild flowers. There was more silence than sound in our days. Prayer was in the air. One felt energized and relaxed at the same time.

Pieper's description of leisure was a perfect fit, with one exception. I returned home eager for work, while the Pieper thesis states: "No one who looks to leisure simply to restore his working powers will ever discover the fruit of leisure." Still, I've tasted the sweetness of the unending holiday, and I'll keep *working* at getting it right.

Ways to Ponder Your Blessings

1. Ponder Josef Pieper's description of leisure as "an unending holiday."

2. Where do you appreciate your human connection to the whole universe? How does it feel?

<œ> *12* <œ>

Advent Inspirations

*T*he season of Advent invites us to look for signs of the Holy Spirit and to welcome all those discernible in the rhythms of daily life.

The Scriptures are a good place to begin looking for the Spirit. The account of the Annunciation, for example, as recorded in Luke's Gospel, offers one of the great Advent meditations. The story has inspired painting, poetry and music from age to age.

God's "announcement" is to a young Jewish woman, immersed in her religious and cultural situation, whose world is turned upside down by the unexpected, unsought message. After Gabriel, nothing is the same for her.

Smaller but no less real annunciations occur in our own lives. They are described by the English scholar, George Steiner, in *Real Presences* (University of Chicago) as a terrible beauty or gravity breaking into the small house of our cautionary being (by and large we humans tend to be cautious).

But Steiner says, "If we have heard rightly the wingbeat and provocation of that visit, the house is no longer habitable in quite the same way as it was before."

Intrusions of the Holy Spirit do not simply rearrange our domestic spheres, they bring unimagined worlds into our "houses" — that is to say, into our lives. So it was for Mary. So it is for ordinary people who are surprised by their capacity for the extraordinary.

—A single woman, never married, adopts a child from an Asian orphanage. She's been inspired by the preaching in her parish church.

—A young couple spend the first year of their marriage as lay missionaries in Central America. They were touched by the witness of visiting missionaries to the Newman Center at their college.

—A middle-aged couple whose five children are grown now serve as foster parents for newborn babies (they have cared so far for 100) until the babies can be adopted. *The Spiritual Exercises of St. Ignatius* led them down this un-planned pathway. The Spirit is unpredictable and totally free.

In her new book *Amazing Grace,* writer Kathleen Norris says the Incarnation (which is what the Annunciation is all about) becomes the place where fear contends with hope.

We all have our daily struggles with fears. Will my child outgrow a particular behavior? Are these worrisome physical symptoms I've been having a sign of impending catastrophe? Am I making a mess of my relationships?

Hope enables us to lean on God, to trust God, to wel-come the peace that appears when we least expect it (much like the Holy Spirit). When Gabriel encountered Mary he told her not to be afraid. When the Spirit inspires our own lives (via angels, perhaps) the message is the same.

Meditate on the Annunciation, and you will notice the scene is one of spare dialogue and deep silences, an environment that makes room for the action of the Spirit.

Early on in the Advent season, arranging a few hours apart in an atmosphere of relaxed silence, one can begin to savor the gifts that God bestows on the earth daily. Trees, berry bushes, birds — all these can become icons of God's winter beauty. The same attention and grateful heart — qualities of savoring — can be applied to family customs: cooking, Christmas cards and music which nourish both body and spirit, and strengthen our human ties.

Advent is also a good time to explore the Liturgy of the Hours, now available in easy-to-follow books suitable for lay people. This ancient form of the Church's daily prayer can also help us to discern the Spirit in our midst. The Advent hymns that introduce the morning and evening prayer are filled with expectations of God's coming to us; the intercessions, too, carry a spirit of hopeful waiting: "Lord, help us to stand watchful and ready, until your Son is revealed in all his glory."

Waiting: This is a major theme in the Church's Advent prayer; the theme also is woven into the fabric of our daily lives. Even with our best efforts to simplify the celebration of the Incarnation, we will still find ourselves waiting.

Grocery lines, hospital emergency rooms, the post office, public transportation: these are ever with us. We can observe the faces of those with whom we wait (faces often reveal the struggles and state of mind of the person) and pray for them. We can remember Mary's waiting, and pray for women who are awaiting a birth. We can recall Mary's "Magnificat" ("He has cast down the mighty from their thrones and has lifted up the lowly") and pray for oppressed people everywhere. Advent reminds us that in some ultimate sense all of life is about waiting.

A good checklist for reflecting on whether or not we are preparing for the Incarnation according to the true Christmas spirit can be found in Paul's Letter to the Galatians. "What the Spirit brings is love, joy, peace, patience, kindness, goodness, trustfulness, gentleness and self-control" (Gal 6:23-24).

This is the perfect Christmas list.

Ways to Ponder Your Blessings

1. Using Luke Chapter 1:26-38, reflect on the "annunciations" in your life.

2. Spend some time reflecting on the theme of waiting in Mary's life and your own.

∽ 13 ∽

Christmas Light

*N*ight comes quickly in the season of Christmas. As we leave offices, schools and shops at day's end and glance into the sky, the evening star hangs on the tip of Venus. I am always glad for these rays of night light.

The Advent prayer of the Church has similar glimpses of light. One Vespers hymn chants these words:

> Creator of the stars of night.
> Thy people's everlasting light
> Jesus Redeemer, save us all
> And hear Thy servants when they call.

The stars of night carry a certain celestial light. But Christmas is surrounded by other lights as well: the lights of commerce and festivity. Unfortunately, for many these lights bring anxiety and distress.

Some years ago I heard a homily that illuminated the reason for holiday depression. The priest spoke about how the outward manifestations of celebration (lights, music, parties) might not correspond with one's inner reality.

If indeed we have something within us that is not rec-
onciled, then the outward merriment rings a false note.
We will feel — and be — disconnected from the celebratory mood surrounding us. Inner darkness will overwhelm the Christmas lights.

The answer, suggested the priest, is to try to reconcile
our own brokenness and darkness. Reflection, confession,
forgiveness: these help light the way through early winter.
Then, released from the burdens of sin and judgment, we
can lift our voices and our hearts in true rejoicing.

Unfortunately, this movement of reconciliation may be
more difficult than we think. The first challenge is to "see"
ourselves more clearly.

One meditation in St. Ignatius' *Spiritual Exercises* centers
on a meditation that envisions the Trinity — Father, Son
and Spirit — gazing on the earth and all who dwell therein. The gaze extends back to the beginning of time and
sweeps right up to the present moment. What we are
asked to do is to see with God's eyes, as it were, scanning
the earth's array of races, occupations, moral behavior,
charity and cruelty.

God gazes on it all and grieves.

The meditation continues with the Triune God deciding that one shall appear among the turmoil and the tribu-
lations and bring redemption into the midst.

Then the meditation continues with the Annunciation
scene. Nestled in the hill country of Galilee one sees the
home of a young Jewish woman. Both she and the
dwelling are filled with light. The archangel Gabriel brings
with him all the light from worlds unseen, unimagined.
Winter nights are not so dark after all.

The question before us is how to move from a field of vision that encompasses all the pain, cruelty, distress and sin rampant in our world to a center of peace and creativity; how to move to the dwelling at Nazareth.

It is not so easy. We too often take our ease in the company of cynicism and narrowness, noise and clutter. Thus we miss the beauty of insight and starlight, and fail to speak words of gratitude and hope.

The Carmelite poet, Jessica Powers, understood this temptation to focus on distress only too well. She wrote:

I tore the new pale window shade with slightly
more than a half-inch tear.
I knew the Lady would be shocked to see
what I had done with such finality.
I went outside to lose my worry there.
Later when I came back into the room
it seemed that nothing but the tear was there.

There had been furniture, a rug, and pictures,
and on the table flowers in purple bloom.
It was amazing how they dwindled, dwindled,
and how the tear grew till it filled the room.
The Tear in the Shade

We are too ready to lose sight of the flowers and furniture and character of the room and see only the tiny tear in the shade. When that happens the bright lights of Christmas glare rather than illumine. They appear as harsh intrusions in our lives.

But if we can turn our gaze from the tear — from all that is wrong in our own worlds and in the larger world

— and instead carefully notice the moments of generosity and charity that constantly appear (but are ignored, unlike the tear), we have a chance of joining our own inner lights with those that decorate our town squares, our offices and homes.

Some practical ways to see with the eyes of Christmas include:

—Unclutter the space of Christmas. By that I mean allow time to concentrate on the people who are gifts in our lives. This will likely mean "doing" less, but "being present" more.

—Experience periods of silence during the Advent and Christmas season. Rising a half hour earlier to be alone, remembering that out of the silence came the Word, can change the texture of an entire day.

—Remember Nazareth and the light that still emanates from that historic meeting of Gabriel and Mary whenever darkness threatens to overwhelm one's spirit.

—Seek out sacramental confession and reconciliation services.

—Give thanks for starlight, inner light and the multicolored lights of Christmas.

Ways to Ponder Your Blessings

1. Think of a time when your inner life did not correspond with a celebratory mood. How did you reconcile this and find peace?

2. What are some of the ways that you have found help to "see with the eyes of Christmas" all year?

Part 3
The Communion of Saints (and Angels)

A saint is a person so grasped by a religious vision that it becomes central to his or her life in a way that radically changes the person and leads others to glimpse the value of that vision. . . . The saint helps us to understand new and different ways of living out the implications of the Gospel.

LAWRENCE CUNNINGHAM,
The Meaning of Saints

Tobiah went to look for someone acquainted with the roads who would travel with him to Media. As soon as he went out he found the angel Raphael standing before him, though he did not know this was an angel of God.

THE BOOK OF TOBIT 5:4

- Martyrs: A Certain Kind of Love
- Brother Roger of Taizé
- Catherine of Genoa: A Saint for Our Time
- Ordinary Saints in Stained Glass Windows
- John Courtney Murray, S.J. — A Bridge Between Church and State
- From Worlds Unseen: Messengers and Guides

❧ *14* ❧

Martyrs:
A Certain Kind of Love

*D*uring a recent lunch with several women involved in Catholic higher education, a college theology professor said her students, mostly 18 and 19 years old, were not much interested in her subject — except for one topic. Martyrs capture their attention. They were truly impressed that someone could care so passionately about something or someone as to offer up one's own life.

We usually think of martyrs as those who have died for their religious beliefs. The towering figures of first and second-century Christianity come to mind, of course, those very people who so astonished the young college students. Who would not be impressed with Polycarp or Felicity or Ignatius of Antioch?

For example, I never hear the story of Polycarp without being deeply moved. When brought before the Roman authorities and told his life would be spared if he would renounce Christ, his humble response was simple and direct: "I have served him for 86 years and he has never

73

done me harm. Why would I deny him now?" Polycarp's words "He has never done me harm" have served as a mantra for me in many a difficult situation. These early martyrs — and others through the centuries of Christianity — vividly demonstrate the depth and power of being in love with God.

That "being in love" might lead to physical death, as with Polycarp, (or Jesus for that matter), but it might lead to other forms of sacrificial love, and in fact does in the lives of many ordinary people.

The first meaning of the word "martyr," with its Greek root, is witness, meaning affirm deeply held principles by word or example. The twentieth century is filled with such witnessing.

I think of women (and some men) who marched, fasted and went to jail, during the early years of the twentieth century, in order to bring to public consciousness the injustice of denying women the right to vote. Many if not most of the women suffrage leaders were motivated by biblically rooted religious conviction, to sacrifice their comfort, their time and energy — and even their safety — for the sake of righting a wrong which was directed against a whole class of human persons. I remember how my mother held these women in reverence.

I think, too, of the many American students who, in the 1960s, boarded the freedom buses en route to dangerous situations in many southern states. Black and white students together, joined by clergy of different faiths, gave witness to the principle that civil rights belonged to all regardless of race. These young demonstrators openly showed their reliance on God's strength. They held meetings in churches. They prayed for courage and guidance.

They sang hymns during their marches. And when some of them were killed and mutilated they preached forgiveness and peace. Their steady, daily martyrdom awakened the conscience of a nation, and in many cases, lowered the walls between religious denominations. Catholics, Protestants and Jews discovered permeable borders in the service of God and humankind.

Sometimes sacrificial love and witness are hidden from public view, but nevertheless affect the wider community. Karen and David (mentioned in Part II) have raised five children, and they are now grandparents. For over a decade they have taken foster babies into their home, usually newborns, caring for them until they are ready to be adopted. They estimate they have cared for about one hundred babies. Several years ago a small toddler was given into their care. Her mother was deemed mentally unstable, but social services believed that she would be able, eventually, to care for her child. After a year, the child returned to her mother, but shortly thereafter social services once more removed the child. Karen and David stepped into the breach. Within a year adoptive parents were found for the child. That arrangement also failed, and once again the child returned to David and Karen. This time the foster parents prayed for guidance and for willing hearts to follow the leadings of the Spirit. Their prayer and discernment led them to a life-changing decision: to adopt the child. They could not bear to see her rejected again. This was two years ago. In late middle age this couple is witnessing to the insight of Thomas Aquinas that love generates itself, spilling out in ever-widening circles. In this they mirror the steady stream of *caritas* which flows from God the Father and sustains all of creation.

Many stories of contemporary martyrdom are hidden, like that of David and Karen. Often it is not until years later that we learn of the suffering and sacrificial love. This is the case with many lives — and deaths — associated with the Holocaust. A visit to Yad Vashem in Jerusalem illuminates (literally, with candles) the deaths of a million children killed in the Holocaust. Their names are read aloud as visitors grope their way through the dark, the only light being the distant flickering candles of remembrance. The whole experience re-creates the fear and disorientation that the children must have felt as they were taken from their parents and sent alone into the unknown. The children of the Holocaust echo the story of the children slain by Herod around the time of Jesus' birth.

Elsewhere at Yad Vashem is the Garden of the Righteous which consists of groves of trees, each one planted in memory of a Gentile who risked his or her life to save a Jew during the Nazi reign of terror. The names of the righteous, along with their country, are reminders that courage and integrity and deeply held beliefs have not disappeared from earth. Martyrs walk among us, live in our neighborhoods, ride the subways, pray in our churches — and their presence makes all the difference. They witness to the truth that Love never fails (1 Cor 13).

Ways to Ponder Your Blessings

1. Why do you think that martyrs capture the attention of young adults and how can we encourage their interest?

2. Who are the martyrs in your life? How can you support them?

❧ 15 ❧

Brother Roger of Taizé

A young woman I have known a long time confided to me recently that she longed for some contact with the mystical strain in religion. She was considering Zen.

As we talked it became clear that she wanted a point of stillness, a place of contemplation where God would seem more present. She didn't think — or know — that the direct experience of God was available in the Christian tradition.

This young woman is not unlike young people everywhere who like the young St. Augustine are restless for God. Sometimes they cannot even name the one they long for, but they can name that which stirs their hearts and prods their search.

John Haught, a Georgetown University theologian who teaches undergraduates, says in a book called *What Is God?* that young people, educated in the scientific method, use terms like *freedom, truth, depth* or *trust* to describe their deepest values. Haught thinks these qualities provide hints about the nature of God; young people can be helped to make the connections between these values and the God who is hidden.

It is important to realize, I think, that often young people use non-religious language to describe profound religious realities. Their search for meaning must be honored.

The ecumenical community of Taizé honors this search. The brothers of Taizé see it as their role to listen with care and compassion to young people groping for words to express their hopes and fears.

Listening is the first step in reconciliation.

A half century ago a young man from Switzerland, who was to become Brother Roger, began the Taizé community. He had no idea then that young people from all nations and races would regularly come in great numbers to the monastic community, looking for Christ even if they did not know the name.

For years I had heard about Taizé, located in France near the ruins of the ancient Benedictine monastery of Cluny. I was familiar with Taizé music and chants. I knew that a small group of brothers (the groups are called fraternities) lived in New York City. Years before I had read *Struggle and Contemplation*, by Brother Roger, a journal kept in the months of preparation for a council of youth.

But not until the responsibilities of my work expanded to include youth and young adult ministry did I come to know firsthand the spirit of Taizé.

One summer I journeyed to the tiny village in the Burgundy hills where three times a day white-robed brothers from different nations and different religious denominations gather in the Church of Reconciliation for prayer. They are surrounded by young people, who kneel or sit before several icons that grace the church, illuminated by candlelight. (At other times of day, the white robes give way to blue jeans!)

When I was there, Brother Roger sat with children of the village, one of whom — a boy of nine — was the cantor. The melodies of the famous Taizé music rose in praise to God. Scripture was read followed by silence so that the word of God could enter the deepest recesses of the heart.

The silence was deep and respectful. At evening prayer, Catholic priests rose from the community at the appointed moment, recognizable by their stoles. Young people slowly rose, one at a time, to seek the sacrament of reconciliation.

Brothers, too, stood at the edges of the community, available to those not of the Catholic community who wished to share something of the heart — a burden, perhaps, or a newly kindled desire for God.

One day I joined Brother Roger and the brothers for lunch under the trees, ancient trees that line a much used pathway. Prior to lunch we met in the little house that has been home to him for well over fifty years. During the Second World War Roger, who was then a seminary student assisted and accompanied Jews and others in danger from Nazi persecution to find their way to the Swiss border. Many spent a few nights with him in the house. Perhaps these years of danger and hope shaped his unique vocation to pray and work for unity among all peoples. For if Taizé is about anything, it is about unity. The community is intentionally ecumenical and intentionally interracial.

It also draws on the richness of the past and the promise of the future. Traditional monastic rituals, including frequent communal prayer throughout the day and silence as a foundation of that prayer, are woven into the fabric of the community's life. But the brothers are open to "the call" to bring their prayer to other places throughout the world. They call their "meetings" *pilgrimages of trust on earth.* The key word is trust. Brother Roger often offers meditations on trust. He reaches out, personally, to the young people who come searching, leading them to trust a little bit more, to allow the Holy Spirit just a bit more room.

Now in his eighties, Brother Roger's age sparks speculation about the future of Taizé. He, however, does not speculate. The community belongs to God, and Brother Roger practices the trust he tries to engender in others. "That little springtime" (Pope John XXIII's description of Taizé) is entirely in God's providence.

At the beginning of the nineties I explored with the brothers some way that we might collaborate on behalf of young adults. The brothers suggested a *Pilgrimage of Trust on Earth,* week long occasions of prayer and community, a version of the regular summer weeks in Taizé. India, Hungary, Poland, Paris, England: all had hosted these meetings.

The U.S. bishops' Committee on the Laity subsequently decided to invite the brothers of Taizé to organize a similar meeting in the United States.

Thus it was that in May of 1992, young adults from across America (ages 17-30), and groups of young people from Eastern Europe, Canada and Mexico, met with Brother Roger and others from Taizé at the University of Dayton in Dayton, Ohio. They came together to pray, sing, listen to God's word and learn something about basic Christian communities.

To prepare for this pilgrimage to Dayton, Taizé brothers visited communities and churches throughout the United States, consulting young people and finding a hunger among them for something to hope in. In the Taizé tradition, the prayer and music in Dayton were prepared with great care.

The Taizé brothers have discovered how to create a meeting ground for the young, a place where their questions are taken very seriously, a place were young seekers connect with others who "speak their language," companions who listen as they give voice to their deepest longings. Years later, the University of Dayton and the surrounding churches, continue to pray the Taizé way. Hopefully, my young friend will find something like that.

Ways to Ponder Your Blessings

1. Who are you being called to "listen to with care and compassion"?

2. Let music be your prayer starter today. How can you create an atmosphere of reverence in your home through music?

❧ *16* ❧

Catherine of Genoa:
A Saint for Our Time

When the great spiritual theologian and guide, Baron Friedrich von Hügel, was constructing his master work, *The Mystical Element in Religion*, he chose a comparatively little known saint as the epitome of a fully developed mystical consciousness — Catherine of Genoa. For von Hügel she embodied the integrated Christian life, one immersed in spiritual awareness and outward mission. Although she lived during the early Renaissance (1447-1501), she has an amazing relevance for our times. Her story includes an unhappy marriage and an unusual leadership role for a woman.

Born Catherine Fieschi, she was raised in an aristocratic Genoese family, and at age sixteen entered into an arranged marriage with Guiliano Adorno, a nobleman. Almost from the beginning the marriage was troubled. Guiliano was involved in extra-marital liaisons and Catherine found herself not only lonely and melancholy, but on the verge of despair. Her own family, deeply concerned about her emotional and psychological health, urged her to take an interest in the city's social life. At first she resisted, but finally acquiesced to their wishes.

At the same time that she was honoring a host of social commitments, her prayer life deepened to a profound degree. She was in the midst of what can only be called a total and complete transformation, a conversion of heart, mind and will. The magnitude of her interior changes led her almost immediately to active care for the poor who lived in the slums of Genoa. *Their* life became *her* life. For awhile, she labored amongst them alone. But then one day Guiliano — her separated husband — joined her, an apparent response to a conversion in his own life.

In time, Catherine assumed the direction of the large Pammatone Hospital in Genoa where she and her husband became residents, the better to facilitate their care for the poor. As director, Catherine displayed administrative exactitude, financial thoroughness, and compassionate solicitude. She was known for consistency and integrity.

In 1493 the plague, which decimated much of Europe, raged through Genoa. Catherine was determined to care for all who came to her. She transformed the open space surrounding the hospital into an outside infirmary. There she spent months supervising the doctors, nurses, priests and Franciscan tertiaries who cared for the dying. It was evident to all that she carried within her the light of the world which Jesus spoke of in the Gospel. Others who recognized the light gathered around her to learn. Among them was the founder of the Oratory of Divine Love, a band of laity and clerics dedicated to the reform of the Church through the spiritual renewal of the individual and the care of the poor. These, of course, were the twin pillars of Catherine's own life.

Catherine's inspiration and influence were as varied as her own life experiences. In later centuries, the gentle St. Francis de Sales and the hard driving St. Robert Bellarmine, were guided by the example of her spiritual-apostolic life. Many 19th century Protestant leaders were also influenced by Catherine, including Isaac Hecker, the convert to Catholicism and founder of the Paulists. One may see her statue in the facade of St. Paul's Church in New York City, a sign of the Paulists' reverence for her.

When Friedrich von Hugel was asked why he chose Catherine rather than Teresa of Avila or the "other" Catherine (Siena) as the central figure for the *Mystical Element in Religion,* he replied that he had known her and loved her for many years. Many in the 19th century women's rights movement, a movement with religious foundations, discovered in her an example of a lay woman, whose marriage was troubled, whose psycholog-ical sensitivities led her to the brink of despair, but who nonetheless grew in consciousness of the vastness of God's love, and of her capacity to respond to that love. While her culture had severe limitations regarding what women could do, they were not limited in terms of spiri-tual knowledge, as Catherine demonstrates. That knowl-edge freed her own natural administrative gifts allowing her to successfully lead a large hospital during a time of great crisis in her city. Her life and teaching has relevance for religious feminists of *our* time, women (and men) con-cerned about equality for women *and* about faithfulness to their religious roots.

Catherine understood that the *true* self and God are

inseparable, a way of thinking found in the writings of the Apostle John. This deep, inner identification with the Divine empowered Catherine to a life of creative service; the same is possible for today's *feminists*.

Ways to Ponder Your Blessings

1. Where do you see the mystical in your everyday life? How does a life of active service equate with the mystical?

2. When, to your surprise, have your natural gifts manifested themselves?

～ 17 ～

Ordinary Saints in Stained Glass Windows

Wheeling, West Virginia is home to many beautiful forms of life. Graceful deer weave through the woods; autumn foliage is like fire on the hillsides; craftspeople produce exquisite Fostoria glass; and the Sisters of St. Joseph continue a creative ministry of mercy and love begun well over a century ago. The sisters' story is all there, in the stained glass windows of their motherhouse in Wheeling. It is a history wrought in color.

The windows tell of five St. Joseph Sisters of Corondolet who sailed up the Ohio River from St. Louis, passengers on a flatboat, journeying in response to a request from the bishop to found a hospital in the Wheeling area. The year was 1836. The spirit was distinctly pioneer.

The sisters from Corondolet not only established the much needed hospital, they also began an orphans' school. They knew only too well the needs of the children whose parents had died or were critically ill. They were women who, in the nineteenth century, noted the signs of the times (and of place) and acted accordingly. The spirit of Vatican II — that is, the spirit of God — was evident in the lives of prayer and service observed by the pioneer sisters. Before long some Wheeling women joined the sisters and several of the original founders were able to return to their Corondolet home. They left behind a small, poor community of women who were rich in commitment to their two-fold mission of nursing and teaching. And the pioneer spirit continued to stir the hearts of some of them to follow new paths.

In the late nineteenth century Sister Bernardine, described as quiet and subdued, began a ministry to prisoners in the local jail; her concern stretched as far as the state penitentiary and beyond that, to the governor's office. Just and fair treatment of the prisoners was at the center of Sister Bernardine's interests, and part of the justice question was the use of the death penalty for a variety of crimes, not all of which could be considered capital. The really amazing part of this late nineteenth, early twentieth century prison ministry is that Sister Bernardine fitted it in "after school." Religious life, at that time, was more highly structured than it is now. Every moment was accounted for; there was no "slack time." When did Sister Bernardine visit the jail or write to the governor? Clearly, in the spaces of her busy life.

Today's Catholic women, lay as well as religiously vowed, are dedicating themselves to a variety of social ministries, from shelters for destitute and battered women to pastoral care for the imprisoned, from hospitality to new immigrants to lobbying for peace programs. And so much more. But it is important to remember the pathfinders, the women who have gone before us — women like the sisters of St. Joseph of Wheeling. They have cultivated the soil of our caring and preserved the seeds of courage, qualities so necessary for responsible change. The women from Corondolet who sailed up the Ohio River may not have thought of themselves as Christian feminists, (a term only recently included in our lexicon), but their graced adventures reflect the qualities of Christian feminist spirituality, which is characterized by mutuality, interdependence and a profound respect for human life.

The stained glass windows at Mt. St. Joseph tell the history of such human mutuality and interdependence. Meditating on them, and on the stories that flow from them, make one pause and consider the possibilities of new horizons of service to life.

Ways to Ponder Your Blessings

1. How is the spirit of Vatican II a pioneer spirit and how can you foster a pioneer spirit in yourself? your family? your coworkers?

2. How does the term "slack time" resonate with you? How can you protect yourself from the "workaholic" syndrome?

❧ 18 ❧

John Courtney Murray, S.J.:
A Bridge Between
Church and State

*T*he taxi driver says he'll never forget him. He picked up his "fare," a Roman Catholic priest, one blustery autumn morning in the mid-sixties. They had engaged in some conversation, an exchange of words whose courtesy deeply touched the cabby, when suddenly the priest slumped over in the back seat and the shaken taxi driver was pushing through New York City traffic, heading for the nearest hospital. The right action, of course, but too late. John Courtney Murray — Jesuit priest, theologian, expert advisor at the last session of the Second Vatican Council, architect of the Church's contemporary concept of religious liberty — was dead.

It would seem that some men and women have a particular vocation to bridge disparate worlds, reconciling that which seems eternally at odds. Such a vocation was John Courtney Murray's. His task was clearly not limited to teaching Jesuit scholastics at Woodstock College; it ventured much further than the boundaries of a typical mid-century theologate. This man's vocation was to build a bridge between the unpredictability of American democracy and the tightly held order of the Roman Catholic church. Many think he succeeded with extraordinary grace.

John Courtney Murray was quintessentially American. He was born to parents of Scottish and Irish descent, and his father — a lawyer — died when he was twelve. He grew up in Queens, New York and attended St. Francis Xavier, a Jesuit high school in Manhattan where his primary extracurricular activities were debate and dramatics. Throughout high school he intended to study medicine, but at sixteen he decided to join the Society of Jesus. He went through the usual rigorous Jesuit training and was ordained a priest in 1933. After post graduate work in Rome, Murray became a professor of dogmatic theology at Woodstock College, the then Jesuit school of theology in Maryland. His speciality was the theology of the Trinity.

In the early forties, Murray became editor of *Theological Studies*; he also served as an associate editor of *America*. In time he became recognized as the theological spokesperson in America for what may be termed the new interpretation in Catholic Church-state theory, a constructive restatement of the relation between church and state in the modern world. In some ways it seems that Murray was surprised by the fact that his work on church-state relations moved to the center stage of his own life. The debate between conservative and progressive Catholic thought seemed a long way from the reflective discourse about the nature of God to which he was accustomed. On the other hand, because Murray situated much of his argument in the primacy of conscience, theology remained the foundation for his growing understanding of the meaning of freedom in church-state relations.

Traditional Catholic thought tended to wed church and state in a juridical union, but Murray moved from the abstract to a person-centered approach. The citizens of a state who are also Catholic must be allowed to worship God in accord with their consciences, he said. And it is this assertion of the primacy of conscience and the respect of the state for conscience that is the foundation of John Courtney Murray's thesis on religious liberty.

Because John Courtney Murray's theories suggested that the role of the church in a pluralistic and democratic society is not to make use of the government for its own ends but rather to guide the Catholic citizenry in putting into practice in their political and civil life the principles of their religion, his critics abounded. For awhile he was forbidden by Church authorities to publish these modern views. It was clearly a surprise to many, then, including Fr. Murray, when he was asked to serve as a peritus or official advisor at the final session of the Second Vatican Council; it was Cardinal Spellman of New York who arranged for Murray to be present at the Council for this all important session. There the final version of the Declaration on Religious Liberty was hammered out and promulgated. One easily sees the influence of Murray on this document. The human person and the human conscience are the points of primary reference. The great American experiment in the separation of church and state is also evident.

The document on religious liberty is very brief, but like

the Declaration of Independence it inspires the exploration of liberty and its meaning in many different contexts. John Courtney Murray himself noted in the document's introduction that "The children of God who receive this gift from the Father through Christ in the Holy Spirit assert it within the Church as well as within the world, always for the sake of the world and the Church." These words are particularly poignant as the church tries in our time to accommodate a plurality of theological opinions within the unity of the faith handed down over the centuries.

Perhaps we need to invoke John Courtney Murray's intercession to help us meet the challenge of pluralism and unity not only in our country, but in our church as well. We need Murray's spirit of civil discourse and courtesy to even begin.

Ways to Ponder Your Blessings

1. In what way do you see yourself as a bridge builder?

2. Describe an experience of conflict of conscience regarding the living out of your Catholic faith? How can Murray's thesis on religious freedom help?

⊸ *19* ⊸

From Worlds Unseen: Messengers and Guides

*I*n the opening scene of Shakespeare's "Hamlet," a ghostly figure appears. But the characters who first "see" the ghost are not fearful. They presume he has something important to communicate:

"Stay, illusion! If thou hast any sound, or use of voice, speak to me."

The ghost is silent, though, and drifts off, but only for a time. Indeed, in his critical role he is a force for justice — some would say revenge.

Ghosts, spirits, things unseen: These attract the interest not only of literature's devotees. The hit film of the summer of 1990, "Ghost," was about a young man murdered on the streets of a big city while strolling home with his girlfriend.

The audience saw his "spirit" leave his body, move through the preliminaries of joining the spirit world but remain on earth long enough to attend to the unfinished business of justice for his murder and his girlfriend's protection.

People enjoyed the film's classic conflict between good and evil, with the good spirits winning. They also warmed to the treatment of life after death, which gave a fictional slant to traditional beliefs.

Beyond theater and films, surveys indicate that people are seeking spiritual experience and spiritual development. Young people especially are eager to be part of some spiritual stream.

From participation in prayer groups and meditation alone or with others, to more eclectic practices like vegetarianism and Eastern disciplines, it is evident that many people hunger for contact with worlds unseen. Clearly, we do not live by bread alone.

The challenge for Christians is to reopen the door to things unseen, with all the safeguards and guidance tradition has garnered.

Take angels.

These beings are present in the story of God's relationship with humanity from the beginning.

An archangel, Michael, took God's cause in hand in the creation account. Another, Gabriel, communicates God's plan of salvation to Mary. Raphael accompanies Tobiah on what could be a most perilous journey.

I remember hearing at Masses during the time after Pentecost, readings from the Book of Tobit. One could not help but notice how attentive congregations were as this most human story of love, fear, trust and risk was recounted. After each reading I found myself praying for a Raphael-like companion for my own journey.

Most Catholics of a certain age learned of guardian angels at the same time they learned their letters and numbers — as little children.

Classrooms were graced with images of the winged friends, and "Sister" taught us to "listen" to their guidance. Some people later put aside for awhile recognition of angelic presence, thinking the devotion was only for children.

The American artist, Thomas Cole, beautifully depicted the ambivalence over angels in a series of four paintings called "The Voyage of Life." In the first, "Childhood," the artist shows a guardian angel and a boy at ease together.

The second painting, "Youth," finds the angel at some distance as the youth sets off in a small boat. "Manhood," the third painting, has the angel rather remote in the background. In "Old Age," the man and his angel are making their way toward a new shore together again.

I must confess my own ongoing interest in and devotion to angels. Some thirty years ago, a German monk advised me during a confession to foster devotion among all in our household to the guardian angels.

I suppose in quiet ways that happened. As one of our daughters was about to be confirmed years ago, she chose "Ruth" as her confirmation name. I thought perhaps she had read the book of Ruth. But she said no. "Ruth" was her guardian angel's name.

I asked, "How do you know?"

"I named my angel," she replied.

One Sunday long ago, just as our family was gathering for dinner, there was a knock at our door. A stranger from out of town announced he had seen us at Mass, was waiting for someone to fetch him, then asked if he could wait with us. He wanted to discuss the homily.

It happened that the priest was having dinner with us. We asked the stranger to join us.

We never learned his name, or we couldn't remember, and to this day everyone, including our now adult children, speaks of the time an angel came to dinner.

What is remembered is the laughter, the excellent conversation about the things of God and a presence that shed light and warmth in different ways.

These intermediaries known as angels prepare us to encounter the glory of God and shield us from rushing in where they themselves fear to tread. They inhabit the farthest realms of heaven, but also the deepest territories of the mind.

The poet Jessica Powers wrote about them this way in "Ministering Spirits":

Know that your soul takes radiance from the angels.
She glories in these creatures of her kind
and sees herself thus lightsome, free as wind.
She stands abashed when the flesh rudely brings
its homage to these pure intelligences
and tries to crowd their beauty into bodies
and weight their grace with gravity of wings.

Ways to Ponder Your Blessings

1. Use the Book of Tobit to pray with today. Think of a time when a Raphael-like companion came to your assistance in a time of need.

2. Are guardian angels only for the young?

Part 4
The Challenge of Change

*Let nothing disturb you; nothing
frighten you.*

  All things are passing.
  God never changes.
Patience obtains all things.
  Nothing
is wanting to one
who possesses God.
  God alone suffices.
  ATTRIBUTED TO ST. TERESA OF AVILA

- The Grace of Letting Go
- Women and Changing Horizons
- Contemplation and Aging
- At Home: A Catholic Look at Equality
- Community and Continuing Conver*sion*

∼ 20 ∼

The Grace of Letting Go

*P*acked away in my memory bank is the line from Annie Dillard's long ago bestseller, *Pilgrim at Tinker Creek,* that more or less reads as follows: at the end of life not please, but thank you. The line is set in the context of recognizing that the world belongs to God, and that all of us are God's guests here. And just as a decent guest says to the host after a lovely dinner party "thank you" instead of a greedy "please," so too Ms. Dillard hopes to do at the end of her days. I like the stance of gratitude for all that has been given that this "thank you" conveys. I like, too, the lightness. No grasping here. One is reminded of the English spiritual writer, Evelyn Underhill, who counseled that in prayer there must be "no craving, clinging or grasping." Rather, she said, one should simply turn to God and let the Creator of the universe transform us. As we do so over and over again, we adhere to God, something quite different from grasping.

The origins of tithing have roots in this stance of gratitude. From earliest times the religious impulse has been to return to God a portion of the first yield of crops and live-stock. Before tithing became an imposed church tax, there was a quality of pure offering in the act, a sign of trust in God's providence.

One wonders if there is something ingrained in the human heart and psyche that urges us to offer gifts to God even though so many theologies describe God as beyond needing anything. What is the impetus for such offerings?

I believe the need to express gratitude for life — as did Annie Dillard — is one factor. When I watched a friend line her dead husband's coffin with the finest linen she could find, I knew she was thanking God for her loving companion. When African Christians bring birds and fruits and works of art to the altar of worship during Mass they do so in joyous dance and with enthusiastic drum-beat. Their thanksgiving overflows.

But, I suspect there is another dimension, besides "thank you," to the act of offering. It is the impulse to freedom. When we let go of money, or other forms of wealth, or treasured keepsakes, it is a way of declaring freedom. One is not bound or defined by things, even good things. I learned this when we moved from a house I've loved, a house that had been home to our family for over a quarter of a century. I used to declare I would be buried in the back garden, so attached was I. But we left and I am at peace. Equally surprising was my desire to gift our children with family treasures: china, silver, paintings inherited from various family branches. The Irish Beleek cookie jar went to one; the Lenox bowl to another. The children at first wondered about all this, but there seemed to me a rightness in the shedding. I felt lighter and freer.

Tithing works this way, too. It creates a light touch in

the money world, while building a strong base in the realm of faith. One discovers over and over that there really is enough when one simply lets go.

But what if you have very little to offer to anyone? The gesture, the "movement toward" is everything. What parent doesn't rejoice over the painted rocks, or woven potholders, or abstract drawings that their children create and offer to them?

Two true stories from Asia illustrate what I mean. Both stories were told to me by a Sri Lankan priest, now dead, shot while saying Mass in his troubled country. One story is about a mother who lived on the streets of New Delhi with her five children. The priest's religious community invited the family to sleep in their courtyard at night, hoping they might be a bit safer from marauders. The first morning of their ad hoc tenantcy, this same priest brought food to the mother; he knew she was hungry, and in worse physical shape than her children who seemed to be managing better. The woman took the food, bowed to the priest in a gesture of thanks, and then distributed the food to her children who sat in a circle. An old man happened to walk by at the same time. He paused to gaze at the little circle. The mother went to him, offered him food before taking any for herself. The priest watched this drama in reverence. He told me that for the first time in his life he truly knew the meaning of Eucharist.

His other story is similar. He and a Buddhist monk traveled together through the villages of Sri Lanka taking a census on behalf of the government. It was in a period of relative calm and peace. People were amazed to see a Christian priest and a Buddhist priest walking, eating, sleeping together like brothers. The people saw this as a definite sign of God's presence, and so they were forth-coming with needed information. The two "priests" often shared a meal with a village elder. On one occasion they were stopping in the hut of a very poor man who had very little rice, but who insisted on sharing it with the itin-erants. The man prepared four bowls rather than three; the fourth he took down the road a way, and simply hung it on a tree branch. It was, he said, for one who might walk by, one poorer even than he.

These stories are not only about freedom; they are also about connectedness, about the intimacy of the Body of Christ.

Jessica Powers knew the power of offering, even if one had little or nothing to put forth.

> The gesture of a gift is adequate.
> If you have nothing: laurel leaf or bay,
> no flower, no seed, no apple gathered late,
> do not in desperation lay
> the beauty of your tears upon the clay.
> No gift is proper to a Deity;
> no fruit is worthy for such power to bless.
> If you have nothing, gather back your sigh,
> and with your hands held high, your heart held high,
> lift up your emptiness.
>
> *If You Have Nothing*

Gratitude, freedom, connectedness. All are gathered into the daily offering of our Eucharists, and they spill out again into the streets of Delhi, the woods around Tinker Creek, our homes and offices and schools. *Deo Gratias.*

Ways to Ponder Your Blessings

1. Today pray with Annie Dillard: "at the end of life not please, but thank you."

2. Have you found that "there really is enough when one simply lets go"?

❧ 21 ❧

Women and
Changing Horizons

*O*ne ritual of my childhood home was Mother dressing up on Election Day. Special jewelry, fur coat, a beautiful hat all were donned as she awaited my father, who would drive them to the polls.

Mother told me that she remembered when women could not vote. She was celebrating progress.

As a graduate student in the '50s — later in the '60s — I was well aware that certain fields had a "women's quota:" law and medicine, for example. Today, those professions are wide open to women.

That, too, is something to celebrate.

Becoming conscious of the equality of women and men involves a process of continual discovery at deeper levels.

In 1995, women and issues of equality were center stage as the world prepared for the U.N. Fourth World Conference on Women, held that year in Beijing, China.

All during 1995, Pope John Paul II focused attention on the church's concern for women's dignity. He emphasized that while they are different, men and women are undeniably equal.

From his annual World Day of Peace message promoting women as "teachers of peace" to his universally well-received *Letter to Women* issued three months prior to the Beijing conference, to his *Appeal to the Church on Women's Behalf* in September 1995, the pope made women a priority.

Especially notable were a series of reflections the pope gave publicly during the Angelus prayer. Brief and to the point, they covered a range of women's concerns.

In one, Pope John Paul said there is an urgent need to achieve real equality for women in the workplace. He specified equal pay for equal work, protection for working mothers, fairness in career advances and argued that mothers should not be forced to work outside the home against their will.

In another Angelus message he stressed the importance of women's greater involvement in public life. "How great . . . is the role they can play on behalf of peace, precisely by being involved in politics," he said.

And he called for enhancing women's roles in the church, "making full use of the ample room for a lay and feminine presence recognized by the Church's law." He specified areas open to women such as theological teaching, the forms of liturgical ministry permitted (including service at the altar), pastoral and administrative councils, diocesan synods and particular councils, various ecclesial institutions, curias and tribunals, and pastoral care of parishes. Those, he said, are ways of providing for the "feminine genius" in the church's pastoral life.

The pope was opening wide the door of the Church's

mission and ministry, and inviting women to enter! In fact, Pope John Paul consistently has called for mutuality between men and women, where each adheres to the vision in the biblical Letter to the Ephesians (5:21), which insists that all Christians are to be mutually submissive to one another.

The pope recognizes that not all in the Church have honored the principles of equality, and he calls this a reason for regret.

But consciousness usually grows at a patient pace. Each new awareness opens yet another door for women. And every open door presents challenges.

A challenge for the Church is to find ways of inviting and encouraging women's leadership. Since women are not ordained in the Catholic Church, how can their experience, their unique sensibilities, their "genius" (in the pope's language) find a place in decision-making processes?

The pope, in his 1989 apostolic exhortation on the laity, urged that women be involved in the preparation of missionary and pastoral statements. One way to ensure this involvement is to have women working in diocesan and national positions where such documents are developed. Another way is to consult women at all stages of development.

Many believe the time has come for competent women to represent the Church at national and international meetings where participation is not linked to ordination. We had a good example of what can be done with the appointment of Mary Ann Glendon of Harvard Law School to head the Holy See's delegation to the Beijing women's conference. Glendon ably presented the Holy

See's views and as a wife and mother ably articulated women's concerns.

The local churches also are making room for the feminine presence in more personal and private ways. For example, there we find a growing number of women who are spiritual directors and retreat leaders — one way the "genius" of women is being expressed.

A current challenge, according to some theologians, is to identify the charisms needed for the 21st century and the ministries to put these charisms into action. Women surely will have significant roles to play in this regard. How will this challenge be met? The Bishops' Committee on Women (National Conference of Catholic Bishops) in their recent statement *From Words To Deeds* made the following commitment. "We pledge to explore new ways in which we can effectively advocate on behalf of women. In particular, we will give special attention to two areas. First, heeding the Holy Father's call 'to pay attention to the whole question of how women's specific gifts are nurtured, accepted, and brought to fruition in the ecclesial community,' we will educate ourselves about the particular needs, concerns, and gifts of women and how women's gifts can be affirmed and incorporated into church life. Second, we will explore what new forms of church leadership may be needed for our time and take steps to ensure that women are prepared for these as well as existing leadership roles."

The needed insights are not likely to emerge suddenly, whole and entire. Probably they will be discovered bit by bit.

But we can still celebrate each new awareness, each new commitment. That's how I remember my mother, who remembered and celebrated the brave women who secured for her the right to vote.

Ways to Ponder Your Blessings

1. Think of a woman — family member or friend — who you see as a role model for women in the church today. What are the charisms she possesses?

2. Is there a feminine presence in your parish community? How can it be encouraged and celebrated?

❧ 22 ❧

Contemplation and Aging

Developmental psychologists — at least those who recognize the spiritual dimensions of the life cycle — alert us
to the contemplative possibilities of aging. By this they
mean that contemplation is not only an act or a particular
form of prayer, but is also a constituent of life at different
stages. Contemplation, defined as awareness of our union
and intimacy with God, becomes as present to us as our
breath which is, of course, a clear sign that we are alive.
Growing old, then, can also mean living contemplatively.
Along with bi-focals, one acquires a lens for seeing the
sacred in the ordinary rhythms and events of daily life.

Loss is one way the contemplative capacity is cultivated in later life. With the addition of every decade of life
comes the diminishment that may come as an illness.
Whatever the form, we find ourselves rearranging priorities. Instead of measuring our life in accomplishments
quantitatively, aging invites us to pause, and to savor the
gifts of God. St. Ignatius of Loyola teaches that it is not
knowing much that satisfies the soul but knowing

interiorly the one true thing — our pearl of great price. A friend who suffered a mild stroke, and whose eyesight was affected for a few months, described his new condition as "mulling over things" — thinking, reflecting, praying, aware of the gift of his existence — these welled up in him as books and newspapers were off limits for awhile. With physical vision restored, the challenge now before him is how to keep "mulling."

Loss comes in other ways as well. Retirement sometimes creates an identity crisis if one's self concept and worth has been closely tied to a role or to status. A church leader I know, who discovered that his title, his support staff, his office, the invitations he received and the honors awarded him had been propping him up for years, literally collapsed when he retired. He had to discover anew — or perhaps for the first time — who he really was. Who is this "irreplaceable person" (a phrase often used by Pope John Paul II to describe the uniqueness of each individual), he wondered? With medical treatment and loving spiritual direction, he gained personal balance and a new perspective on the value of his *being,* a value not dependent on what he's able to do or what others think of him. He sees now that walking the New England beaches, observing birds in flight, reading poetry, moving through each day with deliberate attentiveness — all these constitute his song of praise. This man's late-life journey reflects a passage from Thomas Merton. "Many poets are not poets for the same reason that many religious people are not saints: *They never succeed in being themselves. They never get around to being the particular poet or the particular monk they are intended to be by God. They never become the person or the artist who is called for by the circumstances of their individual lives. . . They waste their years in vain efforts to be some other. . . ."* This transformed church leader is *now* being himself, and rejoicing.

In our golden years, Jesus' teaching to "consider the lilies of the field" acquires ever deeper meaning. A certain leisure accompanies age, which while making one more conscious of limitations, also reveals the dimensions of inner freedom. I can roam about the fields of my life, stopping here to savor this memory or that photograph, recalling particular blessings, seeing the paths of my life, with difficult turns and sometimes steep ascents, from a totally new perspective.

Many writers on the spiritual life note that the prospect of aging can be frightening. Celtic theologian, John O'Donahue, connects the fear to a greater stillness and solitude that one's life takes on, and he argues that these facts need *not* be frightening. The solitude of later years provides an antidote to the restlessness of earlier periods. In youth and middle age we are often thinking about and planning for the future — and missing the present moment. Elderhood opens us up to the present but it also opens us to appreciate the past with all the experiences that have shaped and prepared us for this time of silence and solitude.

Jesuit theologian, Karl Rahner, connects the fear with a keener sense of the nearness of death. The fear, he writes, is not incongruous with being a faithful Christian. "I think that fear of death belongs to the nature of death and I am not of the opinion that a Christian must necessarily die as a Stoic or as a Socrates. I can confidently meet death and also accept the fear of death in a final confidence and surrender [to God]." Taken as a whole, Rahner (who lived to be eighty) viewed old age as a grace not given to every-one. Rather it is to be seen within the unique vocation of each person.

The grace of age is not simply for our individual bene-fit. The Christian community can benefit from the wis-dom of its elders; it can also provide support and love so that the natural solitude of aging will not disintegrate into alienation. Inviting the elders to help the community sift through the plethora of information and to locate the essentials can benefit both the elder person and the com-munity and elders who bear the institutional memory can help us locate necessary anchors in the streams of tradi-tion.

Finally, we do well to remember that creativity does not dry-up at mid-life. For example, the later paintings of Cezanne bring us to the edge of mystery. And when Vladimir Horowitz returned from exile to give a concert in Moscow, Russians wept in the streets as his passionate music poured forth from the concert hall. Horowitz was eighty-three.

Solitude, community, creativity, freedom — all are aspects of a contemplative life. They build on the founda-tions of all that has gone before: prayer and worship, aes-thetics and responsibility, suffering and surrender. As we age we do well to remember the insight of St. Therésè of Lisieux, namely, "tout est grace" — all is grace. She, who died in youth, still transmits to us the wisdom of the ages.

Ways to Ponder Your Blessings

1. Consider the "benefits" and "fears" associated with aging in this essay. What are some examples from your personal experience?

2. What are the conditions which foster "mulling time" and what are the benefits to you, your family, the church, the world?

❦ 23 ❦

At Home: A Catholic Look at Equality

*F*ew people these days argue (at least publicly) in favor of the inequality of women and men.

Intellectual assent to equality abounds in principle. The trouble arises when individuals or institutions examine their actions.

Then the discussion's focus is usually on women, since, historically, men held dominant positions in our various social arrangements. How are women treated? How do men behave? What, if anything, needs to change?

Family life is not exempt from such examination.

An important document of the U.S. Catholic bishops, "A Family Perspective in Church and Society," presents a vision of family life in which a primary task is *to serve life,* which includes developing each family member's potential.

Obviously this relates to children's education and spiritual formation. It also relates to men's and women's changing roles.

In the span of one generation, we saw a movement of women from the home into the workplace, motivated not by economics alone. As women became more educated, they expected to exercise their professional skills.

Add to that motive the pressures of a global economic slowdown and one sees why two incomes became the norm in so many households. With that came struggles over the dimensions of shared responsibility at home.

A functional equality of men and women became more evident as men grew more adept at caring for small children, preparing meals, doing laundry.

But the equality of men and women reaches deeper than household duties. It is about how power is shared and influence felt. These questions are probably the source of much of the tension in many contemporary marriages.

In Christian life — and Christian marriage — power is viewed through a special lens. Creativity infuses the idea of power in marriage. Generating new life and bringing human persons to birth is a distinctive mark of this creative power. Catholic tradition regards this as a sharing in divine creativity. It is one area where equality is tested.

How will decisions about family size be determined, for example? A goal of natural family planning, which requires the joint action of husband and wife, is to deepen dialogue about the meaning of marriage and the relationship in shaping a vision for 'this' family.

Creatively sharing power does not end with the birth of children, however. Deciding which traditions and values will be passed from generation to generation is another example of sharing power.

Perhaps in the husband's family Christmas Eve is a time

of feasting and gift giving; Christmas Day a time of relaxation and rest. Perhaps in the wife's family Christmas Eve has the quality of a vigil, impatiently awaiting the next day's celebration. How these two "views" of the holiday get blended will say much about that family's practice of equality.

Other decisions also are important. The underlying question is how will important decisions be made.

While it is widely accepted in Western cultures that marriage is a partnership, (a covenant, says the church), it is, I believe, a unique one. Our teaching calls for *mutual submission* — not dominance by either partner — of each to the other. There is enormous freedom and power in this.

What the second chapter of the Letter to the Philippians says about how to relate to one another in community also applies to families.

"There must be no room for rivalry and personal vanity. . . Look to each other's interest and not just your own. Let your bearing toward one another arise out of your life in Christ Jesus. For the divine nature was his from the first; yet he did not think to snatch at equality with God."

Such mutuality does not come easily. Life together at home reveals our flaws and emotional neediness, and will require ongoing reconciliation, whose value holds a lesson our world dearly needs.

Christian discernment is needed so that submissiveness does not become one-sided, slipping into oppression — or even abuse — on the one hand, passivity on the other. The U.S. Bishops' Committee on Women condemned using Scripture to condone abusive behavior toward women in a 1992 document titled "When I Call for Help."

It said: "Even where the Bible uses traditional language to support the social order common in the day, the image presented is never one that condones the use of abuse to control another person."

Every marriage is likely to be characterized by physical and psychological differences which result in different traits, interests and talents. *Equality means reverencing the differences and helping each other develop personal gifts.* For example, many women testify that their husbands encouraged them and provided practical support at home when they returned to school to pursue educational goals.

Attention to equality in marriage also is important for children. A spirit of respect and responsibility at home helps boys and girls believe in their own worth and that of the other.

Furthermore, practicing equality at home reaches beyond — to neighborhood, parish, city and nation. For everything is connected and, as St. Thomas Aquinas taught, *love is diffusive of itself.*

Thus, at home we have a chance to practice a way of life that ultimately honors society's common good.

Ways to Ponder Your Blessings

1. The author speaks of "enormous freedom and power" in the Church's teaching of "mutual submission" in the covenant of marriage. Is the word getting out? Is it making a difference?

2. Share an example of "equality — reverencing the differences and helping each other develop personal gifts" — from your own marriage or your circle of friends and family.

❧ 24 ❧

Community and Continuing Conversion

*S*everal years ago a co-worker described to me a monthly gathering of colleagues who all worked at the same church agency. They met in one another's homes, shared a meal, and talked about their work (mostly), but also about their personal lives. It was open to whomever wanted to join the group for an evening, or for a succession of evenings. "Does the group have a purpose other than social?" I asked. "It's for *support*," he replied.

I thought about that, trying to decide whether to accept his invitation to participate. Support? Who and what were being supported, I wondered.

It seemed to me that the individuals were benefitting from social bonds being forged at the monthly gatherings and as they grew in the knowledge of one another, within and without the workplace, they could look for assistance of various kinds. They also served as listeners for one another, to some degree at least. But all the time I had the nagging sense that the monthly meeting was not *support* in any explicitly Christian way. Why? So many of the classic characteristics of Christian community were missing, the most notable being some growth in consciousness about the need for conversion.

One of the principal reasons people commit themselves to carve out time from a busy, often over-burdened schedule, to meet regularly with other Christians is because they know that Christian growth can only be sustained in the company of fellow sojourners.

As Christians strive to be faithful to God's call in their lives, whether that be a more attentive family life, the development of an ecologically sound lifestyle, or service to the poor (or some combination therein), it quickly becomes evident that the task is too large and the energy is too limited "to go it alone." A community of persons also trying to follow the call to a more committed Christian life is needed for renewal and for *remembering* to be faithful. In the group described at the beginning of this essay, no larger purpose seemed to hold the people.

Also missing was prayer. In communities of genuine Christian support some form of prayer will ground their coming together. The prayer need not be elaborate but it should be intentional. One group I know which meets regularly for prayer, a common meal, life sharing and study (and often some corporate action) applied their basic format to a Labor Day Picnic. They had gathered on that occasion for a picnic, simply to enjoy one another. But their corporate identity was so tied into prayer that first they spent a half hour in meditation and intercession about each other's work, focusing on how they saw their work as a response to God's call.

Another missing piece was what I would call a spirit of gentle correction. To uncritically and unquestioningly receive the stories and accounts of problems and decisions from one another — as apparently the first group did — is to give (to some extent) unconditional approval to the behaviors of others. A Christian support group measures the members' stories against the Christian story as recounted in scripture and in the tradition of the church. That tradition includes "testing the gifts" within the community (as in the First Letter to the Corinthians), and "the correction of companions" as spoken about in the Letter of James.

As people seek support for their work problems, their home situations, their vocational questions, their responsibilities as citizens of the world and of the church, I sense that what they are really seeking is help in clarifying the Christian approach to these problems. Should we attempt to reconcile with hostile co-workers? How can a parent deal with a rebellious teenager? How can we participate, as Christians, in the nation's social agenda, and in the international order? These and many more questions shape the horizons of our concern. The support of our companions helps us to see the horizon, and decide what changes we must make.

Support for ongoing conversion is found not only in groups, but in one-to-one relationships as well. In both contexts certain principles of conduct apply:

1) *Truthfulness.* If support is about helping one another then we need to find ways to recall that it is the truth that makes us free. Simply, we state the truth of our situation, and we receive the truth of others' counsel and wisdom.

2) *Prayer.* At some point Christians acknowledge that "talking through" is only a partial response to the critical (and not so critical) questions of human life. The spiritual energy of prayer — adoration and thanksgiving, petition and intercession — releases the energy of guidance and healing, and also the willingness to forgive and to begin anew. Conversion and prayer are intertwined.

3) *Study.* We — all of us — need resources so that we continue to grow and to change if needed. Supportive people introduce us to books, programs, processes and people that can initiate and maneuver change, for example, a twelve-step program, or a retreat, or a counselor.

4) In addition to support that challenges and stretches us, we need people to comfort and console us, who provide us with loyalty and respect, who are trustworthy and discrete. Add to this mutuality, which holds it all together.

By now you may have recognized in this notion of supportive community the qualities of friendship. No one has written more eloquently about this most prized relationship than Aelred of Rievaulx.

Aelred was a Yorkshire monk who lived in the 12th century. He is best known for his treatise on spiritual friendship which he understood to be on both the natural and the supernatural plane. Frankness and not flattery, generosity and not gain, patience in correction, and constancy in affection he saw as the marks of a genuine friendship. Aelred's own words deserve a hearing:

> In friendship which is the perfect gift of
> nature and grace alike, let the lofty
> descend, the lowly ascend; the rich be in
> want, the poor become rich; and thus let
> each communicate his condition to the
> other, so that equality may be the result.

It is this kind of support that helps us grow into the full stature of Christ.

Ways to Ponder Your Blessings

1. Reflecting on the variety of groups that you have been part of, how have one or two of them fostered your growth as a Christian? What characteristics do these groups share?

2. How do you rate your relationships based on Aelred's "marks of a genuine friendship"?

Published by Resurrection Press

A Rachel Rosary Larry Kupferman	$4.50
Catholic Is Wonderful Mitch Finley	$4.95
Christian Marriage John & Therese Boucher	$4.95
Come, Celebrate Jesus! Francis X. Gaeta	$4.95
From Holy Hour to Happy Hour Francis X. Gaeta	$7.95
Glory to Glory Francis Clare, SSND	$10.95
Healing through the Mass Robert DeGrandis, SSJ	$8.95
The Healing Rosary Mike D.	$5.95
Healing the Wounds of Emotional Abuse Nancy Benvenga	$6.95
Healing Your Grief Ruthann Williams, OP	$7.95
Heart Peace Adolfo Quezada	$9.95
Life, Love and Laughter Jim Vlaun	$7.95
Living Each Day by the Power of Faith Barbara Ryan	$8.95
The Joy of Being a Catechist Gloria Durka	$4.95
The Joy of Being a Eucharistic Minister Mitch Finley	$5.95
Transformed by Love Margaret Magdalen, CSMV	$5.95
RVC Liturgical Series: The Liturgy of the Hours	$3.95
The Lector's Ministry	$3.95
Behold the Man Judy Marley, SFO	$4.50
Lights in the Darkness Ave Clark, O.P.	$8.95
Loving Yourself for God's Sake Adolfo Quezada	$5.95
Mustard Seeds Matthew Kelly	$7.95
Practicing the Prayer of Presence van Kaam/Muto	$8.95
5-Minute Miracles Linda Schubert	$4.95
Season of New Beginnings Mitch Finley	$4.95
Season of Promises Mitch Finley	$4.95
Soup Pot Ethel Pochocki	$8.95
Stay with Us John Mullin, SJ	$3.95
Surprising Mary Mitch Finley	$7.95
Teaching as Eucharist	$5.95
What He Did for Love Francis X. Gaeta	$4.95
You Are My Beloved Mitch Finley	$10.95
Your Sacred Story Robert Lauder	$6.95
Your Wounds I Will Heal Faricy/Rooney	$8.95

For a free catalog call 1-800-892-6657